CHAPTER 1

"Aima! Aima!" Mrs. Ibiye Richardson, who had been discussing with the boat driver, cried out as she alighted from the boat and her little girl was nowhere to be found. Visibly agitated, she paused and reflected. "Where on earth could she be?" she asked herself. She heard the voices of little children on the shore and hastened her steps, hoping to find her among them. She was disappointed and she turned back, asking people on her way if they had seen her child.

Above, the clouds chased each other as they prepare to water this part of the earth. The sound of thunder could be heard amidst flashes of lightening and rising wind. Sensing an imminent storm, Ibiye's mind went into overdrive, as she continued her search.

Early in 1948, Mr. Frank Richardson had married a young girl from the next compound in Abonnema. By 1956, their seven children were all born: Inyingi, Dabo, Belema, Angel, Emmanuel, Aima and Moty. Of the lot, only Dabo and Emmanuel were males. Due to their early exposure to the outside world, their parents went to the extreme to bring them up in the traditional way. The Richardsons were a hardworking and responsible couple; the family never lacked. Aima was her parents' favourite child and they took special interest in her; they pampered and accommodated her temperament.

Aima was born in the colonial days to Mr. and Mrs. Frank Richardson in 1955 in the coastal town of Abonnema, a beautiful island and one of several in the Niger Delta region of Nigeria. The inhabitants of the Island had early contact with European explorers in the shape of traders and missionaries, who came to the region by sea. Consequently, the Island and her people benefited from the impact of European culture. The natives adopted European customs, religion and names. English names became fashionable even when parents could not speak the language, or did not even know the meaning of such names. More especially, English names became mandatory for those who wanted to be baptized – young or old, because the white missionaries considered native Kalabari names to be for unbelievers. Initially, trade and communication between the natives and the white men was difficult as they resort to gesticulations and drawings. Over time however, the natives learnt and spoke some passable English, the level improving as people started attending school.

The natives were predominantly fishermen, although the womenfolk occupied themselves mainly with the gathering of periwinkles, oysters, or fishing for shrimps and crayfish. Some remained at home as full housewives and engaged themselves in petty-trading or ran liquor bars. These bars came to life mainly at nights when the men got back from the sea or other form of work they've been engaged in. At such times, they would gather around with friends and drink local liquors such as kai-kai, a locally brewed gin, over a bowl of fresh fish, seasoned with lots of pepper and served hot.

The sixth child in a family of seven, Aima Richardson, even as early as four years of age, already had a mind of her own, and exhibited great intelligence. Though quiet and shy, she was by no means timid. By the tender age of seven months, she had developed her own vocabulary. One could call it baby babbling but each word actually made sense. What is more, she always made sure her babbling was understood. For example, if she needed her pet dog, she never settled for a toy or any other item. She would blab, "No! No! No!" at every wrong suggestion made, till her dog was produced. If she needed milk, she made sure it was given to her. She would frustrate any effort at giving her anything else until the right thing is produced.

Aima learnt much by observation, and as she grew older, her curiosity grew with her. She once asked her mum why her dad's chest was flatter than hers and why she wore a bra while her dad wore a singlet. She explored her environment and daydreamed. Sometimes she would pretend she was a queen; the trees and plants are her subjects, while the sea and the rivers were her territory.

Moty was Aima's youngest sister. She got her name as a result of the interactions between the whites and the natives. When she was born, one of the white men described her as "mouthy" because she had thick lips. From this singular statement, she became known as "Moty." She was a true "little African beauty." Frank, their daddy, traveled to Europe for studies with the encouragement and help of their white friend, Mr. Jack Straw, after she was born.

By January 1958, life in the village became too difficult for Ibiye. What with seven kids and little or no financial support from anywhere! Moreover, since her husband left to study abroad, she had not heard from him. Communication was by mail and took a lot of time to arrive. Ibiye decided to save and relocate her family to the city of Port Harcourt. She believed they would have better opportunities there and with hard work, she could improve on their standard of living. She committed herself to this conviction and by the end of the year, she had saved enough money to pay not only their fare to Port Harcourt, a city about 30 kilometers from Abonnema, but also rent a sparsely furnished one bedroom apartment in a building with a row of single rooms facing each other and separated by long corridors. Residents even shared kitchens and bathrooms. There was no privacy in these lodgings as neighbours saw themselves at every turn. One had to queue to use the common facilities. Ironically, the children saw it as an opportunity to make friends.

The voyage was an awesome experience for Aima, since it would be the first time she would be traveling by sea. No sooner had they alighted from the boat than Aima set about counting the trees – her favourite pastime. She had just begun counting when her mum called out to her.

"Aima! Aima!"

"Yes mummy!" she answered, startled.

"What have you been doing?" Questioned her mother with a stern look. "I have been looking all over the place for you."

"Nothing mum," she answered, feigning seriousness.

Suddenly, she saw a car for the first time. In fact, she had only seen cars in pictures and wondered what on earth they might be.

Ibiye, apprehensive of the approaching storm, gathered her children and luggage around her and frantically waved down a cruising taxi cab, but the driver ignored her flailing arms and drove on. In desperation, she hailed another one as it passed and was luckier this time as the driver stopped. After a lengthy haggle over the fare, the family boarded the vehicle and was driven into the city.

The city people looked different from the villagers. Aima, the ever observant one, even noticed that some kids wore elevated shoes, popularly known as high-heels. The best footwear she ever owned was a pair of rubber slippers. Since Ibiye and her children arrived on

Sunday at a time people were returning from church service, everybody looked good to Aima's four-year old mind. The little girls had on elegant dresses with colourful decorations on their long hair. Neither she nor any of her sisters had ever had long hair as their mother always cut their hair. Besides, plaiting or braiding of hair was considered as luxuries by her. She also reasoned that cutting of hair is a sure way of preventing lice.

As soon as the Richardsons settled down, Ibiye, with a portion of the money she had saved, enrolled the children in a nearby government primary school. Although the children had missed the first term, they were fortunate to be admitted for the second. The school year ran from September to July of the following year, with each academic year comprising three terms. They benefited from the country's free Universal Basic Education scheme. The government schools admit new pupils even in the middle of the session.

Ibiye decided to take advantage of the opportunities that urban life offered her. She reasoned that all she needed was basic education to enable her read, write and speak well. With this in mind, she enrolled for evening adult education classes at a private educational center, just a stone's throw from her house. "At least I will be able to discuss with my husband when he returns even if it won't be at the same level. Frank would surely be proud of me. He will be glad to take me to occasions where current and enlightened issues are discussed..." she mussed.

Fortunately for her, on October 1, 1960, Nigeria got her independence from Britain. This created new vista of opportunities for Nigerians. By this time, Ibiye could just about read simple sentences. Through privileged information from a neighbour, she heard of vacancies and applied for work in the State Library as a cleaner and was fortunate to be employed. With the job, came accommodation. The colonial masters had built staff quarters for all government workers. The senior staff lived in a special area called the GRA (Government Reserved Area). The junior workers reside in quarters while the military dwelt in barracks. The junior staff quarters were mainly small, semi-detached buildings with in-built conveniences. Ibiye was very happy to move out of her "face-me-I-face-you" single rooms.

Her new job does not pay much, but it was by far, better than what she had had earlier. As a cleaner, she had much time on her hands. Her typical day started at about 5 am. She got up early to prepare the children for school before proceeding to the office. She started work at 7 am and had to ensure that the offices and the reading rooms were cleaned before 8 am when the Library opened to the public. Once the office opened, she remained in the waiting room in case any of the officers would need her assistance. By 3 pm she was done for the day and would eventually be at home an hour later. She knew that money is most productive when put to task, and so she invested the remainder of the money she had saved into a small scale business. Back home, she traded; retailing cold drinks, biscuits, sweets, toiletries and other provisions. It was actually the kids who handled the sales from a little kiosk at the front of the house. All Ibiye does was to replenish the stock as often as was necessary before setting off for her adult educational programme.

Initially, she attended fashion and design classes on Sundays at a nearby fashion house after church service, familiarizing herself with the rudiments of the fashion trade since her work with the library board afforded her time to improve on her education and skills. When she was less busy, she did her class assignments and read her books. And since hard work has its rewards, she excelled in school and in three years, had completed her primary education, obtaining the First School Leaving Certificate in flying colours. With prudent management, she saved just enough to buy a sewing machine with which she can practice at home and in rare instances, get a customer.

Because secondary schools did not run evening classes, Ibiye decided to stop her education and concentrate more on her work at the Library. She also spent more time with her kids and tailoring. It was now 1963 and Inyingi, her first daughter, was already thirteen years old. Dabo was a year younger while Moty, the baby of the family, was seven.

Everybody contributed his or her quota to the well-being of the family. Inyingi was the first to join her mum in the tailoring business. Her work was to fix buttons and hem or tack the finished clothes. Dabo also assisted in the tailoring and sales in the kiosk. Angel was the assistant chef. She helped prepare the less complicated meals like garri or rice. Ibiye did the purchasing of food items in the market and the complex cooking. The rest were assigned to whatever they could conveniently handle.

Ibiye had indeed made progress since her husband traveled overseas to improve on his education. She had secured a job for herself and accommodation for the family, which is by no means, a mean feat. She had taken all necessary steps to educate herself and her children, but in her heart, she was worried and unhappy. The thought of her husband's absence and his inability to communicate with her since he traveled abroad, tortured her. Each time she remembered him; she would shudder and frantically shift her attention to other things.

"No word from Frank! Something must be wrong, or is he dead with all these horrible tales making the rounds? How could he be alive and not have sent even a letter?" She bemoaned.

Many disconcerting stories were being told of life abroad. How men ended up marrying white women and settling there. This they did because once they got married to citizens, they too, would become citizens and be able to enjoy the rights and privileges due to bona fide citizens.

In spite of all these stories, Ibiye remained steadfast and rejected all advances made at her by members of the opposite sex. Just as she never believed for one moment that Frank would betray her love or forget her and the kids, she refused to believe he was dead. Every night she prayed for him; for his safety and well-being, beseeching the Almighty to bring her husband home.

CHAPTER 2

The time was 11:15am, the date February 24, 1964 and location, Mrs. Richardson's house – tailoring section. On this day, Inyingi was frantically working on a dress, when she suddenly called out:

"Mummy, these buttons you gave me for Mrs. Boro's dress don't fit."

"Inyingi, you mean you have not finished working on her dress?"

"I am on the last button," she informed her mother.

"You know how troublesome she is. I am expecting her at any moment. She needs the dress for a cocktail party tonight. You know, she is one customer in whose bad books I don't want to be listed."

"Mum, you will certainly be because of these red buttons on her pink dress."

"I thought they were pink buttons."

She stepped forward to take a closer look as Inyingi lifted the dress.

"I thought so too, but you know you gave them to me at night and the lights were dim."

Mrs. Richardson became nervous.

"Oh! What do I do now?" She wondered. "Fast, get me pink buttons from the container!"

She picked up a razor blade on the top of the sewing machine and hurriedly cut off the red buttons as her daughter went for the right buttons. Inyingi presented two sets of pink buttons to her mother.

"Mum, I'd rather prefer these. They are flat and a little bigger than those other ones."

"You are right my daughter," responded her mother as she collected them. "Fast, thread another needle. We must finish before she comes."

The two hurriedly began to fix the new buttons. After a short spell of silence, Inyingi looked at her mother and said:

"Mum, Mrs. Boro knows how to enjoy herself. How I wish she would take me to some of those parties she frequently attends!"

"You have to wait till you grow up. My daughter, things are not generally, what they seem as appearances can be deceptive. Mrs. Boro confided in me that cocktails are very boring. She said people spent much at parties but all they do is stand around and gossip. At cocktails, it is important to be in the right crowd and not to say the wrong things and of course, to laugh when a big functionary or official tries to make a joke, even when it is not funny. You see, as a lady, you mustn't eat much. In fact, Mrs. Boro said she eats at home before attending any occasion, so she doesn't go there and disgrace herself."

"How can I eat before going to a party?" Asked Inyingi. "I thought parties are for eating, dancing and making lots of noise."

"Not cocktails," corrected her mother. "They are not like birthday parties, my dear daughter."

Inyingi at last fixed the last button and gave the dress to her mum who collected and flapped it to straighten and remove dust and tiny cuts of thread and other materials from it.

"I am happy you informed me early enough. It is done..."

A knock on the door made mother and daughter look at each other, smiling.

"Yes, come in," Ibiye called with satisfaction knowing she had finished Mrs. Boro's dress.

The door opened and a young girl of about twenty years of age entered, carrying a big bag. She looked fresh with a glowing skin. When she opened her mouth to speak, she sounded like a European though she looked to be of African descent.

"Can we help you, my dear?" Asked a bewildered Mrs. Richardson.

"My name is Boma. I am from Buguma."

"Our own Buguma!" Inyingi exclaimed excitedly.

"Yes. I was born and raised in the United Kingdom, Newcastle-upon-Tyne, to be precise. I am looking for Mrs. Ibiye Richardson."

"Is there anything the matter?" asked Ibiye. "I am Mrs. Ibiye Richardson. Please sit down." She offered, as she entered the house.

The girl took a deep breath and sat down. Ibiye drew her daughter close to herself and held her in trepidation as the girl unzipped the bag she was carrying.

"I'm sorry I didn't come immediately on arrival. I have a letter, some money and other things from Mr. Richardson for you."

As Mrs. Richardson and her daughter looked on, she brought out a big parcel which she handed over to her. She opened her other bag, brought out ten Pounds and a letter which she gave to Ibiye. She offered the big bag and Ibiye took it from her.

"Did Mr. Frank Richardson give you these things himself to give to me?"

"Yes, he did."

"Do you know him?" Questioned Ibiye.

"Of course I know him! We belong to the same Association of Nigerian Students in the United Kingdom."

"How is he?"

"He is fine and doing well. Whenever we meet, we discuss issues in Kalabari. I am married to a Briton – a white man. My engagement party in November was held at Newcastle-upon-Tyne, and Mr. Richardson was one of the guests. It was there I told him my parents insisted that the traditional marriage hold in Nigeria." She stopped for breath and then continued. "Again, I'm sorry I couldn't bring them early. I have been in town since Christmas for my traditional wedding, but I was very busy making preparations for the wedding. In January however, I tried in vain to reach you at Abonnema. I finally met a member of your family who told me you work at the Library Board in Port Harcourt. It was at your workplace that someone gave me this address."

"When are you returning to the UK?" Asked Mrs. Richardson.

"Next week. Your husband has been worried. He had made several attempts to reach you, but since he did not receive any reply to his letters in the past, he pleaded with me to locate you and deliver the parcel personally to you, see how you've been coping with the children and bring him back a reply. Well, I am happy you are sound in wind and limb. I will come back in two days time to see if you have anything for him."

Boma turned towards Inyingi, prompting an introduction.

"Oh, this is Inyingi, my daughter."

"She is such a beauty. Inyingi, how are you?"

"I am fine," she answered shyly, stifling a broad smile that brightened up her face.

"Where are the others?" Boma asked. "Mr. Richardson told us he has seven children."

"Some are in school, others are out visiting friends, you know how children are." answered Ibiye.

She made sure Boma had a good meal and a bottle of soft drink before leaving.

Boma thanked her, picked up her bags and stood up.

"Mrs. Richardson, thank you very much for this hospitality. I am happy I met you and will not fail to tell your husband everything. I will now be leaving for home. I have to travel in four days time. As I said earlier, I will be back in two days in case you have any message for him."

"Thank you Aunty Boma," said Inyingi.

"And thank you too beautiful one. I love the way you help your mum in her work. My dear child..." she paused, realizing she isn't old enough to be her mother, and then continued: "Be diligent in whatever your hands find to do. You never know when you will be needed to repeat it somewhere else."

"I promise to do my best Aunty."

As Boma left, Inyingi jumped up and hugged her mother.

"What does Aunty Boma mean by the word 'diligent'?"

"It means being committed in whatever one is doing in life."

"And how come you know the meaning of the word?" Inyingi asked, laughing.

"I know by asking others wiser than myself, when I don't know the meaning of a particular word."

"Just as I did now?"

"Exactly, and now no more questions, we have things to do."

Mrs. Richardson carefully opened the letter and read:

December 10, 1963

My Dear Wife,

How are you and the kids? I have been thinking so much of you people. I did not abandon you and our children. I don't know what you may be thinking since you have not replied any one of the letters I wrote you. Or didn't you get them?

My first letter as I arrived here was sent through a friend that was traveling to Ghana. I personally posted four other letters and sent other things through friends traveling back to Nigeria. Is the P&T not functional again?

Well, as Boma is traveling to Nigeria for her wedding this weekend and she is from Buguma, near our hometown, I decided to send this letter and parcel for you and the children.

I gave Boma ten Pounds Sterling to give to you. The list of items in the parcel is attached to this letter. I also gave her instructions to bring everything back if she couldn't locate you.

I have successfully finished my education. I am now a medical doctor. I still have a few loose ends to tie up. As soon as I am through, I will come back home. I know you have gone through difficult times.

How are the kids and how have you been coping with them. They must be grown up now. Will they remember me? I hope they are all in school. How are the people in the village — Nne, Papa and the rest? Extend my greetings to everyone.

I pray God to protect you all. I will see you soon. I love you.

Yours affectionately,

Frank

Once again, Mrs. Richardson hugged her daughter as tears of joy formed in her eyes. She blinked and it dripped down.

"Thank you God. I knew he was alive."
The inflection in her voice made Inyingi turn and look at her:

"Mum, are you crying?"

"No, I'm not crying my daughter." She said as she made a frantic effort to hold back the urge. "I am overjoyed." As she saw her daughter's eyes welling up with tears, she said: "This is our happiest moment, don't you think so?"
Inyingi nodded.

"Now let us open the bag."
She saw an attached list, scanned it and then excitedly began to open the parcel in the bag.

Her husband had sent a few clothes for her and the children as well as some toiletries: toothpastes, body lotions, two bottles Armani perfumes and two dozen toilet soap.

Later that day, Mrs. Boro sent a youngster to collect her clothes.

*   *   *   *

In the evening, Mrs. Richardson gathered her children around her and narrated the whole incident with Inyingi heartily contributing. During the process of sharing, Mrs. Richardson made the kids try out the various dresses. When it got to Inyingi's turn, she advised her mother:

"Mummy, you know I was here when Aunty Boma brought these things. I should get more. Besides, I am the eldest."

"Inyingi, how many are there? I will ask your father to send more clothes, now that we have established communication.

Of the lot, only one dress barely fitted Inyingi and she was not pleased.

"Even this does not fit, but I will keep it. Mummy, you will have to compensate me with something else. I will take one of the Armani perfume and..."

"And what?" Her mother queried. "I won't give you any money. I've told you I will ask your father to send more clothes."

The other children were able to get one or two dresses and shirts. They were all happy and made a litany of requests to be sent to their father. They were all happy.

Early the following morning, Mrs. Richardson went to the market and bought some dried fish, shelled melon, bitter leaf and dried periwinkle for her husband. In the evening, she wrote him a letter:

February 25, 1965

My Dear Husband,

May God bless this day. I was very happy when I received your letter, the money and parcel you sent to us. I did not receive any of the previous letters until this one you sent through Boma. The children and I thank you greatly. I thank God that you are alive. God has been merciful to us over this period of time.

We have relocated to Port Harcourt. I now work in the Rivers State Library Board. I work from 8 am to 3 pm, Monday – Friday. The office has a phone. The number is 0804-238900-7. It is very expensive to call from the post office.

Once again, thank you for the money and items you sent. Everybody in the village is fine.

May God continue to keep you.

Your wife,

Ibiye

Very early the next morning, Boma came back as she had promised. After some pleasantries, Mrs. Richardson gave her the parcel and letter for her husband. She also asked Boma to thank him for her.

*   *   *   *

As the family waited patiently for the day Frank would return, Dabo kept getting into trouble. In fact, Ibiye's greatest problems were Inyingi and Dabo. Inyingi, who was now fourteen years of age, had started wearing make-up. She had begun straightening her hair with a straightening comb, while Dabo started blowing out his hair with a hot pick-comb. When Ibiye confronted them, their excuse was that it was easier for them to manage their hair that way. Then she noticed the lipstick, eye pencil, perfumes, and lip gloss. After reprimanding them on several occasions and even seizing these items, she also became suspicious about the source of the money with which these items were bought. At a point, she felt they had been stealing her money, and so instructed Angel, the third child, to keep the cash of their daily sales.

One day, Ibiye felt ill and decided to go home early. When she got home, she noticed a car in front of her house. Assuming the owner had parked in the wrong place, she ignored the car and went straight in. She stopped short at the sight that assailed her eyes; there was Inyingi, sitting on the laps of a young man in her sitting room. When the young man saw her, he made for the door and fled in his car. She later found out that his name was Victor. He was from a rich home. His parents had given him the car as a graduation gift. That day, she gave Inyingi the worst beating of her life.

After this incidence she noticed a change in her and this gladdened her heart. She believed her daughter had repented from her wayward ways but unknown to her, the girl had simply become wiser and more discreet with her affairs.

As for Dabo, the principal of his school had invited her on several occasions for a 'chat'. It had come to the notice of the school authorities that he steals. He had been caught and punished several times for his demeanour and yet remained impervious to cogent reasoning and advice. He would simply not change. He was finally expelled from school in his second year at Government High School. After a frantic search that took its toll on her time and cash, Ibiye managed to get him admitted into another school; the Port Harcourt Boys High School. In the first term of his third year, he got into trouble again. He and his gang had gone to the school buttery and forcefully taken some items without paying for them. They had even threatened to deal ruthlessly with the student buttery attendant if he ever mentioned their names.

In exasperation, the school authorities sent Dabo and his cohorts to a juvenile remand home. Parents were advised to go and bail their kids from there. Since it was a corrective institution, Ibiye after due consideration, decided to leave Dabo there for some time. By the time he was released two months later,

Dabo was a different person. He had completely changed and became obedient. He had even cut his afro hair style. He looked and acted much more responsible and matured.

The next problematic person was Aima, but hers didn't border on attitude; she screams in her sleep due to the recurring nightmares and this usually occurs when she fell ill. The other kids behaved as normal kids of their age would.

CHAPTER 3

The Rivers State Library Board is located along Bernard Carr Street in the Town axis of the city of Port Harcourt. It is a modest structure in terms of size, but what it lacked in size, it made up for in aesthetics. The building is set in a garden environment and a sense of tranquility pervades the atmosphere, affecting everyone that comes into the premises. No wonder there is an amiable co-existence and cooperation among its employees.

On a fine December morning, Ibiye was tidying up the manager's office when she was told she had an international call. She hurried to the phone at the reception, picked up the earpiece from the desk and realized it was her husband. That day was a memorable day for her. Amongst other juicy things, he told her he was coming back home. He had completed his course in the university and will be home for Christmas. Ibiye's joy knew no bounds and she could barely control herself to remain in her workplace.

Immediately after work, she rushed home and prepared her family a delicacy; white rice with chicken and stew for dinner. This was indeed regarded as a luxury in this household as in many others. On smelling the food, the children knew there was good news in the air for their mum never gave them rice on weekdays. They would prod further after the special meal.

Rice was a special treat because it was expensive, although it was not as fulfilling as their usual meal of garri, the staple food for the low and middle class. Garri could either be soaked in cold water and eaten with a spoon or in hot water, stirred into a thick dough and eaten with soup. Almost every family could afford it and it was very fulfilling.

European beverages were scarce and expensive. Milk was like gold to most families. People prefer buying yams and garri to the former. They found these foods more filling as a meal than bread and beverages, which were expensive and yet, could not sustain them for more than an hour or two. To them, bread was a snack and not a meal.

Ibiye made sure there was sufficient food for the family; she kept a small garden at the backyard. But it was not so with clothing and household appliances for the home. They never owned a television set or a stereo. Thank God for free education. The children attended the government public schools. All she had to do was buy their school uniforms, sandals and books. She personally washed and ironed their uniforms, so that they can last longer. Only the first three kids had the privilege of wearing new clothes. The younger ones wore "pass-downs" from their older siblings. Ibiye was lucky that her children are very understanding. They sympathized with her. Their mischievous lifestyle was sometimes, the result of the influence of bad friends or peer pressure. Ibiye was fortunate that no situation got out of hand before her husband returned. Such was the lot of most single mothers in Africa.

After the meal, which they thoroughly enjoyed, the kids became silent, expecting their mum to tell them the good news, but she on her part wanted to raise their curiosity and wasn't forthcoming.

"Okay mummy, what have you gotten to tell us?" Aima, the ebullient one, asked.

"Why do you people think I have something to tell?"

"You don't give us rice to eat except on Sundays so there must be something big you want to reveal," Dabo observed patiently.

"Mummy, have you been promoted?" Inyingi asked, unable to hold back her curiosity.

Again, the house became silent and expectant but their mum took her time before answering.

"No, I haven't been promoted..." She paused for maximum effect and got the desired response.

"Why then did you give us rice to eat on a Wednesday?" Aima queried.

"I got a call today from your dad at the office. He said he would be coming back soon."

"What? When? How...?" They asked astonished.

"He called to say he is through with his academics and will arrive in about two weeks. Yes, my husband is coming home soon." She said with feeling.

Amidst ordered pandemonium that greeted this revelation, she proceeded to tell them the content of the conversation she'd had with her husband.

*   *   *   *

December 20, 1964, was a rainy day. The coastal terrain of Port Harcourt, according to experts, is responsible for the unpredictable nature of the seasons down there. It rained at will. In fact, it is difficult to demarcate between the dry and rainy seasons. All year long, it is either raining or dry. You cannot predict the duration of a particular season. Each time it rained, Ibiye got very sad. She would pray that no one should visit because all around her house would be flooded.

Gone were the days when flooding was unheard of in Port Harcourt. With the influx of people into the city from all parts of the world due to its numerous hydrocarbon based industries, extreme pressure was put on existing infrastructure. Consequently, illegal structures sprung up everywhere in response to a government, inept at handling the developmental pace of the city.

Trees that once adorned every street, earning the city its "garden city" status, had long disappeared to be replaced by concrete fences and shanties built by the invading public on unauthorized locations, especially on drainage paths, thereby, impeding the flow of water.

These, coupled with the littering habit of the inhabitants, contributed to the unhealthy spectacle the city portrays especially when it rained. On such occasions, silt and debris carelessly thrown into the gutters-as drains are commonly referred to, effectively block the drainage system.

In desperation the state government declared the last Saturday of each month a sanitation day. On sanitation days, refuse collectors move around the city and towns in trucks, collecting heaps of refuse for disposal. Everyone was expected to stay back between the hours of 7 am to 10 am to clean up their surroundings, remove the silt from the gutters and stack the debris in readiness for the arrival of the refuse trucks. In this way, it was hoped that the city would be clean. The reverse was however the case. The people who managed to clean their drains never dispose off the debris properly, and the rains eventually wash them all back into the gutters.

At first, Ibiye used to participate with the men in her neighbourhood in the exercise, but when they noticed that no one disposed of the refuse, they stopped. And so, whenever it rained, the drains were blocked and people had to wade through the flood to get to their homes.

To compound the problem, the roof leaked. Both the senior and junior staff quarters were poorly managed by the residents and government officials. Money earmarked for the maintenance of these quarters was misappropriated by officials while the houses were left to dilapidate though the library building fared much better. The staff who resided at the quarters could not use their meager salaries to maintain their quarters. There were also uncertainties surrounding their positions in their places of work. There was no job security. The idea of this being a permanent place of residence became a mirage. Positions usually changed with places of abode.

In view of the leaking roof in Ibiye's house, washing bowls were normally placed at strategic parts of the house, to contain the water that came in through the leaks in the roof.

The day was also a special day for Adamma because she was to be married. She is the daughter of the Amadis, Ibiye's colleague and neighbour. The Amadis were from the eastern part of the country. They were lucky that sixteen-year-old Adamma was getting married. Emmanuel, a primary school teacher, had asked her hand in marriage. Her entire family members were happy because her being married meant there would be one person less to feed. Better still, at least one of her siblings would follow her to her matrimonial home.

Adamma's marriage was a special event for the Richardsons, because she is Inyingi's best friend. Being neighbours and schoolmates, they spent a great deal of time in each others company. They went out, played and attended functions together. Once in a while, they quarreled and kept an unhealthy distance but they eventually always settled their differences. Her marriage was certainly a welcomed development in the family.

Just like Adamma, Inyingi had suitors around her, but her mother insisted she graduate from the university before getting married. This made Inyingi melancholic and sad. She told her mum she could always go back to school after marriage but Ibiye knew better. Ibiye's view was quite different from her neighbours. This was because she was the only female breadwinner on the block. Her female colleagues were either married and staying with their husbands elsewhere, or single and living alone or with their parents. So hers was a peculiar case. Male breadwinners that earned the same salary as she did never had sufficient income to give their children university education. Most of them preferred to train the girls up to secondary school and strived to send the boys to tertiary institutions. For the Amadis, education was not a priority.

Adamma got to secondary school level due to the influence of Inyingi and her boy friend, who was a teacher. Her other siblings did not go beyond the primary school. Ugochi, her younger sister, had been given out to another family as a house help while her two brothers, Chukwuma and Ifeanyichukwu were working as apprentices with a trader in Onitsha in a system called the OMATA (Onitsha Market Amalgamated Traders Association), school system. The system is based on a high-level of trust of both parties.

Onitsha is an Igbo-speaking town in Anambra state of Nigeria. The indigenes are predominantly traders, involved mainly in the import and export of goods and commodities. It is common practice among Onitsha traders to take young boys as apprentices and mentor them for an agreed number of years with the view of equipping them with the practical learning, required to manage their own businesses, when the period of apprenticeship is over.

The internship system is uniform. From the outset, an unwritten agreement is reached between the parents of the intending apprentice and the trader he would be understudying (generally referred to as his master), regarding the number of years the boy would be spending in his tutelage. The generally accepted duration is ten years. In exceptional cases, it would be slightly more or less. There is the occasional incidence were either party defaults, but the process is otherwise, mostly a hitch-free one. The apprentices, usually boys, were not expected to be paid, maintain a bank account or have their private businesses while still in the master's service. These boys were usually only educated enough to count and receive money.

*   *   *   *

Ibiye was in the bathroom, preparing to attend the wedding, when she heard a loud knock on the entrance door. Luckily the rain had stopped, giving her a respite. She continued with her bath, expecting one of her children to answer the door. But the knock became insistent, and this time she wondered who the impatient visitor was. By the time it became irritating, Aima was at the door.

"Who is it?" Aima asked.

"Open and see." The visitor answered.

Aima opened the door and before her stood a tall elegant-looking man.

"Can I come in, my dear young lady?" The visitor inquired, smiling.

"Who are you looking for?" Aima asked, surprised.

"I need to see one Mrs. Ibiye Richardson. I was told she lives here."

From the bathroom, Ibiye had followed the conversation. There was no mistaking that voice; she would recognize it anywhere and anytime. It was almost unbelievable. She called out to her daughter:

"Darling, he is your father."

In her joy, Ibiye almost ran out naked from the bathroom. She quickly threw her clothes round her waist and rushed out to meet her husband. She ran into his outstretched arms and gave him a long hug.

"How did you come?"

"By air. I arrived Port Harcourt earlier, but the airport taxi had to wait for the rain to stop before bringing me down here." Mr.

Richardson explained, still locked in the warm embrace of his wife.

Aima stood there, watching the drama. She was confused as to how she should receive this pleasant stranger – her dad. Ibiye, seeing the confusion in her daughter's eyes prompted her to give him a hug. Like a zombie, Aima obliged without a word. The other kids came out, one after the other, to meet their father. They were all excited, though somewhat bewildered. The man was too neat and polished to be their father. Ibiye took her husband and settled him in. She took him into the room she shared with their daughters. The children brought in his luggage and went to the adjoining room to wait for their parents. The children were confused as to what next to do. They were running late to Adamma's wedding but by instinct, they knew they were not supposed to rush their parents.

After a long while, Ibiye brought out some new clothes for the children to wear to replace the earlier clothes they would have worn. The whole family dressed up to attend Adamma's wedding. Frank decided to attend the wedding ceremony with them. When he returned, he would take a well-deserved rest.

They were the center of attraction at the wedding. People wondered who their gentleman escort was. Some suspected it might be Ibiye's long-lost husband because of the way they held hands. Mrs. Boro belonged to that group of people who knew everything. She was always abreast with the gossip in town, in addition to having the solution to everybody's problems. Her eyes were always watery for trying to pry into other peoples' businesses. She confirmed to the onlookers that the stranger was indeed Mr. Frank Richardson. Ibiye had earlier mentioned to her that her husband had phoned to announce his return before the end of the year. The women were happy for Ibiye. One of them observed that Mr. Richardson was such a refined man. Another of the onlookers remarked:

"Ibiye is so lucky. See how her husband is holding unto her as if his life depended on her."
 "Does he think somebody will steal her away?" Another commented.
Mrs. Boro explained to them that this open show of affection is common practice in the white man's land. They were even more surprised as Ibiye was not dressed in the

traditional wrapper, blouse and head-tie as the other women. Rather, she wore a simple, flowing maxi gown. The kids all wore new foreign clothes, except Inyingi, who had on the chief bridesmaid's dress that had been made for her.

The wedding went well. Frank, Ibiye and the children were too excited to stay till the end except Inyingi, who as part of the wedding train, had to stay till the end of the ceremony. The rest made their way home, chatting excitedly all the way. Even when they got home, they continued the animated discussion, all talking at the same time. Meanwhile, Mr. Richardson kept yawning, a sure sign of his fatigue. At this point, Ibiye suggested they retire to bed early.

The family gathered in the evening after they had eaten and rested with the intention of opening the gifts. Their father commenced to open the packages containing presents he had come back with. Everyone's gift was perfect, except Aima's, who had some clothes that were a bit too small. However, she was lucky that Frank had brought along some other clothes that were of a larger size. These fitted her well. The entire family was gathered in the living room and everyone was all ears, impatient to hear about their father's trip and his life overseas. He started the story in between sips of cold water.

"The trip was quite an experience," he began, "Life over there and here are miles apart. My stay overseas had its hitches, but overall, it was memorable and pleasurable. When I arrived at Port Harcourt from Abonnema, I took a bus to Elder Dempster Shipping Authorities. There I boarded a ship which took about three months to arrive at Liverpool. I then proceeded to London by bus."

"Why did it take so long?" Ibiye asked. "It must have been like the journey of a lifetime," she reasoned.

"It was so because we had to stop over in many countries. We stopped over in Togo, Ghana, Ivory Coast and many other countries. In each country, we rested for a day or two before proceeding."

"How were you sleeping and feeding in the ship?" Aima asked.

"A ship is different from a canoe. Some have many decks... some ships are even bigger than storey buildings. They contain everything. The ship I boarded had bedrooms, which are known as cabins. It also had eating and recreational areas. There was enough space for one to walk around. Each ship is called a vessel and the one I traveled in, was called Queen Amonia. The entire journey was filled with fun. This was because some passengers disembarked while new ones boarded the vessel. We arrived in England by the end of the third month. The sight of London was awesome. Words cannot describe it. Immediately we arrived, we went into the arrival lounge. There my name was announced and I was asked to meet Mr. John Robinson at the information desk..."

"Who is Mr. Robinson?" Asked Ibiye.

"Oh, he is a member of the Anglican Church in Central London. Mr. Jack Straw, his boss, had asked him to come and receive me. The Anglican Church accommodated me the first month I arrived. Thereafter, Robinson assisted me to procure some odd jobs through an employment agency. I did all sorts of menial jobs, from washing of plates in a restaurant to washing corpses in the mortuary. I know you will be shocked that I washed the bodies of the dead, but what else is there for a penniless immigrant. The pay was small, but it was enough to pay my bills..."

"What bills?" Inyingi asked. "Is it not only your house rent and electricity bills you pay?"

"No. You pay for everything there: electricity, phone, air-conditioning, heater, water, cooking gas, garbage collection and so on. The list is endless. It is only the air we breath we don't pay for in the UK. To live well in that country, you need everything. You cannot do without water, phone or cooking gas. Without heating your house, you will freeze to death in winter. Back home, we are lucky; all we pay for is house rent and a few other bills. We don't have winter here, so we don't need to heat our houses. In fact, it was my contact in the mortuary that gave me the idea to become a doctor which was at variance with my original course of study. I made the necessary enquiries, took the necessary examinations and was fortunate to be admitted into the university to read medicine."

"How did you cope with the fees?" His wife asked.

"Is education not free there?" Inquired Dabo.

Inyingi attacked him as she always did when she felt he had asked a silly question.

"Block head, is education in tertiary institutions free here?"

Emmanuel giggled, but was stared to silence by his mum. Her message was unmistakable.

"But it is a different location. Everything works perfectly well there we are told," insisted Dabo.

"Didn't you hear when he said that people pay through their nose for everything except the air they breathe?" Questioned Aima, as she opened a bag containing fruits she bought on her way from the wedding reception.

"Children, children, stop! Let your dad continue his story," Ibiye implored.

"How did you cope with them when I was away? They must have put you through hell," remarked their father.

"On the contrary, they are well-behaved kids. They are just excited at your arrival," she defended.

He paused for a moment to consider her answer, decided it made sense, and continued. "Well, to answer your questions, it was not easy. I worked day and night. Initially, I hardly slept or ate decent meals. In London, you can work flexible hours. You are paid according to the number of hours you work. When I left the church's accommodation, I moved into a small bed and breakfast guest house. The room rates were much cheaper, and every morning they gave me breakfast for free. In fact, that used to be my only meal each day. While there, I applied for a council flat which was for low-income earners or indigent people. I passed their interview and got one."

"Do you need to write exams to own a flat in London?" Asked Aima.

"You have to go through series of interviews for the authorities to be sure they are giving lodgings to the right person. The rent is very low. In fact, it is just a token and yet, it has all the comforts of any regular flat."

"If they are that good and cheap, why doesn't everybody go for them?" A puzzled Emmanuel asked.

"Dunce! Hasn't dad explained to us that one has to go through series of interviews?" Dabo queried and pushed Emmanuel's head.

"Don't use such words," cautioned their father, as he got up to prevent the two boys from fighting.

"I personally will not like to go through all that stress, I will prefer going for a regular flat of my choice." Aima squeezed in as she sucked from an orange.

"That means you have to work hard and make enough money," Inyingi pointed out, in between bites of banana.

"You won't suffer the same fate as I. You are still very young, and won't need to work or train yourself. That is what all my sacrifices are for; to provide for you," he promised as he got up to pace around the sitting room. He noticed the holes in the roof and shrugged his shoulders.

"Why didn't your parents train you, dad," asked Emmanuel.

"Because they did not have the money," Aima replied.

Mr. Richardson was very impressed.

"That was good, Aima. You will certainly be a smart and shiny star someday." Frank fondly commended her, rubbing his palm on her kinky hair.

"What about us, dad?" The other kids fired back in unison.

Before their dad could respond, Aima shot out:

"Oh, jealousy! jealousy! I am the queen, and every other person is my subject."

Ibiye, sensing the growing friction amongst the kids, scolded:

"Will you children keep quiet and let your daddy talk!"

At her admonishment, they were shocked into silence. Never had she scolded them in such a tone as she did now. "Maybe the return of dad was getting to her," they reflected. All the same, an uneasy silence was ushered in.

The night was already far spent and Frank was already feeling exhausted but he made an effort to lighten the atmosphere.

"Children, I'm feeling sleepy now. But let me summarize and we can all go to sleep. I eventually had a one room or self-contained apartment. It is comprised of a room to sleep in, a toilet, a bathroom and kitchen. I stayed there until I got into the university. I was still doing part-time jobs to make ends meet."

"Didn't you have friends? You have not told us anything about them," observed Ibiye.

"Well, initially, I had no friends except the Christian brothers. We only met during church services or programmes. London is not like Nigeria where anybody can knock on your door at anytime. Secondly, things are done differently from us. In London, you have to book an appointment before you visit anyone. Even children don't just cluster outside to play as we do here. There are playgrounds and amusement parks where children play. I spent all my time at work, school and the library. My free times were spent in the library to avoid spending unnecessarily. The more you stay away from your apartment the lesser your bills. You won't be tempted to use the phone neither would you have the heater running. In the library, you enjoy free heat. However, with time, I made friends in school."

Done with the kids, he now turned and faced his wife.

"Darling, you know you are very intelligent. Nobody who sees you for the first time would know you've hardly seen the four walls of a classroom. You must seriously think of going back to school, especially now that I'm back."

Hardly had he finished than Ibiye asked with a hint of false annoyance in her voice.

"Frank, what else do I need a school for? Did you not know that I was an illiterate before you married me? You want to make a mockery of me or do you want me to be in the same class with my kids so that people could laugh at me?"

"No sweetheart, they would say you are very courageous."

"Are you already ashamed of me?"

"Far from it. My exposure outside drew my attention to many things one can achieve through basic education. You know you are the prettiest and kindest woman on the face of the earth. My love for you will never wane."

"What about me?" Aima asked.

"Aima, you are not a woman yet! I love you all. You are the best children in the whole world." He said, visibly perplexed.

Dabo suddenly looked down, unable to look at his father straight in the face.

"Dabo, what is the problem?" His worried father asked.

"What kind of school do you want mummy to attend again, because she…"

"Children," Ibiye interrupted, "It is way past your bedtime and you must go to sleep now. Leave your daddy and I alone. I am the one to inform him of all that had happened in his absence. Now you must all go to bed."

CHAPTER 4

Through his contacts, Frank got a job at the General Hospital, Port Harcourt, as a medical doctor. The hospital gave him accommodation in their Doctors' Quarters and the family moved into the new apartment. It was situated in a better neighbourhood with more rooms. Their standard of living also improved. Better still; the children now attended more befitting schools.

Ibiye got enrolled into another Fashion Design Institute where she would learn the theory and practice of clothes making. She stopped her petty trading to concentrate on her tailoring business and work. Now with a better office space and hired helps, her business took on a new dimension. She only supervised the jobs that came in although; she personally handled the clothes of some high-profile customers like Mrs. Boro and her colleagues that works at the government house.

Ibiye, being well aware of their change in status, took special care to make and maintain the children's clothes and uniforms. Aima had problems which are by no means academic.

The problem with her is her choice of friends and recurrent dreams. Inyingi, on her part, enjoyed this new status to the fullest. Apart from academic challenges, she saw it as an avenue for making new friends of both sexes.

The older children were now in between classes. Inyingi was to take her GCE O'Level examinations the following year. The curriculum in her new school was wider and much higher than her former school. Aima was in her final year in primary school, preparing for the First School Leaving Certificate examination.

Aima, though reserved, was a crowd puller. She was also beautiful and brilliant and was always surrounded by faithful followers. She had a special magnetism about her and her charm won her the hearts of many who were willing to do whatever she wished. From a distance, one could have mistaken her for the leader of a female gang. Being the pretty daughter of a London-trained doctor did not hurt her "standing". She participated in school debates and even represented her school in many such competitions.

She grew prettier by the day. Her beauty was subtle and yet obvious. One look at her confirms her special endowments. She was creative and could endeavour to look stunning in the cheapest of dresses. She was a true African beauty with a mélange of African and European features; full bodied, long legs, great height and a charisma that endeared her to many.

On initial contact, no one would ever know she came from humble origins. She was articulate and has good command of the English language. These qualities she developed by extensive reading and from watching movies. She loved to mimic the actresses in the numerous films she had watched. This habit would pay off in her latter years.

Inyingi, the eldest daughter of the Richardsons, was the black sheep of the family. Or rather, she was a chameleon. She had the uncanny ability of influencing people around her. She also ignored her chores at home. Initially, her parents thought nothing of this habit. Ibiye had gotten used to doing everything for the children. As was customary with firstborns, Inyingi had the habit of sending her siblings on errands and then compensated them for their obedience with gifts. Nobody ever took time to find out how she got the money for these gifts. She also had a wardrobe of simple but classic clothes. It was only when she failed her GCE

O'Level exams that her parents began to get concerned. They enrolled her for extra-mural evening classes which she eventually abandoned for outings with her male and female friends.

Inyingi was bisexual. Her female friends, usually older, showered her with expensive gifts like jewelry, dresses and accessories. Her male friends, contemporaries and older ones supplied her with other personal comforts, particularly cash. She managed to keep this aspect of her life secret. Her parents used to wonder why their daughter kept the company of older women who showered her with gifts.

Once in a while, Dr. Richardson would stop by the school to pick up his daughter on his way from work. Sometimes, he would be lucky to see her and at other times, he wouldn't be so lucky. On her part, Inyingi always saw him. On purpose, she made her lovers park their cars at a reasonable distance from the school. From this vantage point, she always had a clear view of activities at the gate.

One day, Dr. Richardson closed a bit earlier than usual and decided to stop by to pick up his daughter. He waited for almost half an hour but there was no sign of her, so he went to her class. He met a student there who told him

Inyingi had not been at school and that she actually did not have lessons on that day. He reported that he had seen her earlier in the school compound but she later got into a car and left.

Dr. Richardson was confused. When he got home, he confronted his daughter.

"Inyingi, I was in your school to pick you up..."

He did not finish when Inyingi interrupted.

"Really?" She snapped. "At what time?"

"I arrived at 8:30pm and waited till 9:20pm. When I went inside to check on you, your classmate confirmed you had no class today..."

Again, she did not allow him to finish before cutting in.

"I went to read in one of the classes. At about 8:20pm, one of my classmates was leaving and I followed her in her car."

Her father was aware that she had not accounted for the fact she had no business going to school that day since she had no classes, but he allowed it to pass.

That was how she got herself out that time. Somehow, she never got caught, but her parents were now suspicious of her. Her siblings are in the know of her escapades. Though they did not like it, they didn't have the guts to report her. The children in this family were very close. They knew telling on her would cost her much problems. Instead, they prayed that she would one day come to her senses and change her way of life for the better.

Inyingi eventually passed her O'Level, by cheating. She sailed through the university matriculation examinations in like manner. While at the university, she was a part of the crowd known as the "happening" girls. This meant she was always dressed in the most fashionable clothes and kept company with the most popular crowd at school. On campus, she also contested for and won a beauty pageant as the most beautiful girl on campus for that year. Though her parents were not in support of her participation in the pageant, they did not try to stop her. She won prizes in cash and kind. With the cash she had won, the savings from her clandestine activities and a little help from her parents, she was able to buy a car.

She managed to get a job immediately after graduation and moved out of her parent's home. She took Aima and Moty along to live with her, leaving her parents with only four kids to cater for. In a year or two, her brother Dabo, would also graduate from the university, so the financial burden would be less on their parents, she figured.

Inyingi means 'mother' in Kalabari language, and true to her name, she acted like a mother to her siblings. She always had their welfare in mind. Aima on the other hand, means 'beauty'. She lived with Inyingi for several years. Although Aima disapproved of her sister's lifestyle, she loved her dearly. Inyingi always had male visitors and did not think anything was wrong with her way of life. At times, two or more men would visit at once, and at such times, it was the patient 'dog' that ate the fat 'bone'. As was customary in these parts, Aima called Inyingi 'sister,' as a mark of respect.

"Sister," Aima called on a particular day.

"Yes dear," answered Inyingi, looking up from the novel she was engrossed in.

"Why do you keep all these men as friends? The Bible says it should be one woman, one man."

"Aima dear, when I am ready to get married, I will settle down with one man." She replied.

"Weren't you the one clamouring for marriage soon after Adamma's wedding?"

"Aw, that was then. I now know better!"

"But sister," Aima continued, "Why do they still come back even when they meet other men here? I have noticed some even hang around, patiently watching television programmes they don't seem to enjoy."

"Well, my dear, they don't have a choice. They are all married."

"If they are married, why do you continue to see them? And how will their wives feel if they find out?"

"Dear, that is their cup of tea." Inyingi replied, throwing away the novel and reclining on the sofa.

"I really do think you should settle down with a young man and have a family?"

"Well, that is when I see one. A few of them have actually asked me to be a second wife but, of course, I declined their offers."

"How would you feel, if when you get married, your husband keeps a mistress or decides to take a second wife?"

"I will cross that bridge when I get there." She continued. "Meanwhile, Aima you are no longer a baby, you know. It is about time you too started enjoying yourself. Some of my friends have expressed interest in you, but I have always told them you are too young. I guess I would allow them chat you up one of these days."

"Please they should not bother coming, because my answer will be 'NO'. My body is the temple of God, not a toy for men to play with."

"It could be fun you know," said Inyingi. "They play with you, you play with them too."

"Enough! Enough is enough!"

They both burst into laughter.

"I see you enjoyed the joke," Inyingi remarked.

From time to time, Aima attended functions with her sister. She would sometimes also go out in the company of friends or relations. True to her word, she avoided men and never accepted invitations from them; for to her, married men were bad news. They will cause her heartache because they would never marry her and she on her own part, will never agree to share her man. Then, of course, there was the secrecy that surrounded such affairs. It would have to be kept under wraps so that she would not be tagged a call girl. Boys asked her out and she accepted, but once there was any pressure from the guy for an intimate relationship, she would quit. She had her own plans and ideas but nature had another for her.

*   *   *   *

One fateful evening, Aima just back from school, sat on the balcony of their block of flats. They live in a simple but descent middle-class neighbourhood. Such flats were cheaper to rent and maintain. Inyingi had had offers to be kept in more luxurious apartments in high-brow areas of the city, but she preferred keeping a low profile by staying in this area. It gave the impression that she was a hardworking young lady. Neighbours thought nothing of the many male visitors who came by. They took them for relatives or colleagues especially as two or three men usually meet at the same time in her apartment and never created a scene. Inyingi was loved by her neighbours.

As Aima was still at the balcony, she noticed a posh car drive into the street. She wondered what such a beautiful car was doing in their neighbourhood. To her surprise, the car pulled up in their parking lot and a middle aged man alighted from the car. He looked fresh and polished and was completely different from all the other men that called upon her sister. "He must be one of Inyingi's boyfriends," she told herself.

The man walked into the premises.

"May I help you, sir?" She asked from the balcony as she noticed the man looking in her direction.

"Yes, I am looking for Miss Richardson's apartment," he said as he came closer to the front of the balcony where Aima was seated.

"She lives here," she responded and opened the burglarproof – a metal frame that served as a deterrent to thieves.

"I never knew you are so young and beautiful," the visitor remarked. "My friend must be very lucky. How did you know I was coming or has he phoned to alert you?"

She chuckled. He obviously thought she was Inyingi.

"I am Aima. I'm sure you are looking for Inyingi, my elder sister."

"My oh my! I have been babbling without even an introduction. I was carried away by your beauty. I am sorry. My name is Eddy Richmond; I came in from America with a parcel for Inyingi from her fiancé, Mr. Dateme. I am sure you know him."

"No," she replied.

"So then, how are you? Why are you at home and not in school?" He asked.

"I came from school to collect some items and decided to spend the night here."

"Then I must come and visit you in school."

"No," she refused.

"Oh! I understand. You don't want your campus boyfriends to see me. I will pretend to be your uncle."

"That's an outdated style," she smiled. "'Uncle Style' is no longer in vogue."

"Then you will teach me what is in vogue, because I just must see you."

"I actually don't entertain male visitors."

"Then see me as a female," he joked. "Anyway, this is my card and the parcel from Dateme." He handed out both items. "Give me a call when it pleases you, good night. And please give Inyingi my number and tell her to call to confirm that the items from Dateme are complete."

Aima could not sleep that night; she kept recalling the events of that evening. She had enjoyed every minute she spent with Eddy. She loved his sense of humour. In fact, her heart was beating so fast that she thought Inyingi, who was asleep beside her, would hear it. She even wondered why she did not give Inyingi his phone number. Was she afraid that Inyingi would date Eddy and she would be left standing in the cold, lovesick? She didn't believe the rubbish about Dateme being Inyingi's fiancé. Inyingi was not engaged for she does not take any man seriously; she would date Eddy without batting an eyelid even though he was Dateme's friend. Aima began to be worried over the flutter of her emotions over a total stranger. "You are heading for destruction," she told herself. "This man must be married; besides he is much older than you, and you do not belong to the same social class. 'Be wise.'" she told herself. "He was simply being friendly towards you or he could be a Casanova – the use-them-and-dump-them type. Is that the kind of man you want to loose your virginity to? Come on, be wise." She admonished herself.

Aima decided to forget the handsome stranger who had caused this upsurge of emotions in her. She gave Inyingi the complimentary card in the morning, claiming she had forgotten to give it to her earlier.

True to her character, Inyingi called Eddy to thank him and invited him back saying she wanted to send a note to Dateme. This he did, just before he made another trip to America. Despite his busy schedule, Eddy came with the hope he would see Aima once more. Since their first meeting, he had hardly slept. He understood her plight; youth, innocence, inexperience and timidity. She was not his regular type, but something about her kept drawing him to her. Unfortunately for him, there was no sign of Aima the day he visited and he deliberately did not ask of her. He figured that if he wanted to date Aima, he would have to play smart. He did not want to arouse Inyingi's suspicions.

After three unsuccessful visits to the house in the guise of one errand or another for Dateme, he decided to formally invite Inyingi to his place. He asked Inyingi to come with her sisters. Inyingi went with only Aima since she knew he had already met her. They arrived at his house on schedule.

"Are you all here by yourself?" Inyingi asked Eddy.

"Yes. I forgot we had a function to attend this night and I asked my wife to go with the kids, I will join them later."

At the mention of his wife, Aima developed butterflies in her stomach and became unusually quiet. She could not even enjoy the meal that he had specially prepared for this occasion. She felt very uncomfortable and in dire need of some privacy.

"Excuse me sir, please where is the lavatory?" Aima asked.

That was the moment Eddy had been waiting for.

"I will show it to you personally."

As they walked, he moved closer to her.

"Please, call me. I know we cannot talk here, in the presence of your sister. I arranged this meeting because of you. If you don't call, I will visit you at school."

"This is blackmail." She said, but inside, she was exhilarated.

That was how it started; a friendship that gradually blossomed into love.

CHAPTER 5

Richy, as he was fondly called, was raised by his father and his father's younger sister, Mabel. For one reason or the other, Aunty Mabel had refused to get married. No man was good enough for her. Her standards were very high and sometimes, unrealistic. Transparency and honesty were of utmost importance to her.

Richmond grew up without the love of a mother. He was told his mother died giving birth to him and since he heard this, he was never truly happy. His only memory of her was the pictures his dad had in their family album. He was the only child she had for his father. Her death left Richy's dad so heartbroken that he initially refused to remarry. He had strings of mistresses who invariably struggled to be the wife of the house. Ironically, Richmond had looked very much like his late mother. He would have easily passed for a younger version of his mum had he been a girl.

It was this resemblance that made it difficult for his father to stay under the same roof with him. His resemblance to his mother reminded him too much of his late wife and the circumstances surrounding her death. He unconsciously blamed Richmond for the demise of his wife.

After much counseling from the clergy, friends and family, Mr. Richmond Snr. finally accepted to remarry. His pastor made him realize his wife's death was destined to happen and nobody should be blamed, certainly not the little boy. He reminded him that after all, God is sovereign and could therefore do anything that pleased Him.

He married Rosaline Dede. Rosaline was kind and sweet-natured, but because of the impression her husband had created about his son, she couldn't bring herself to love him, no matter how hard she tried. It was for this reason she insisted he called her Aunty Rosa and not mummy. She could not think of being a mother to an evil child, one who had killed his own mother at birth.

Richmond saw his step-mum as a tough person. Because his dad never had time for him, Rosa represented his mum and dad and what a mean example she was! She deprived Richy of any luxury and he had nobody to complain to. Each time he needed something, like a pair of shoes, his dad would insist he took his request to Aunty Rosa first. She only granted his request if she stood to benefit from it; otherwise, she would refuse and that was it.

Every disappointment, they say, is a blessing in disguise. Richy grew up to become a tough, disciplined, hardworking and determined young man. He left home with his father's consent after his O'Level. His father was kind enough to give him a bed suite to stay in and to employ him as a junior clerk in his hotel. That way, Richmond had the opportunity to study, when admitted into the university, and worked while on vacation. With the salary he earned, he paid for his tuition.

Immediately he graduated from the university, he married his sweetheart, much to his father's chagrin. His action put pressure on the already strained relationship between himself and his dad. Richmond justified his actions by saying that he wanted to settle down as soon as possible and start the family he never had. His father, on the other hand, felt Richmond should have had more experience with women before rushing into marriage. Unknown to Richmond, his wife, Vera, was one of those girls who dated elderly men for money. But if he had disclosed this to his son, it would be exposing his own secret life. How could he tell his son he indulged in threesomes in hotel rooms or that he attended pajama parties, and above all, that Vera belonged to that life as well? To his surprise, Vera and Richmond lived happily for four years. In this period, they had two sets of twins, all four were boys.

One day, without any explanations, Vera moved out of the house, abandoning the children. At first Richmond thought it was a big joke. He believed she would come to her senses soon and come back to them. But before long however, he got to know she had relocated to America. Despite her actions, Richmond was still willing to take her back should she make up her mind to return. He really loved her and was not ready to remarry.

She never wrote or phoned but people saw her and told him about her. At the time he met Aima, Eddy Richmond already had a live-in lover, Constance, who everybody called his wife. Although Constance did not have any children for Richy, she had had two sons and a daughter from a previous relationship. So together they had seven kids. Constance knew quite well that if Vera should return, she would have to move out. That was the understanding between them. Richy and Constance were parents to the seven kids. Constance had quickly changed her children's surname and hers to Richmond. Richy warned her of the implications of her illegal action and her answer was that it was just a name and could be dropped at anytime if the need arose.

In truth, Constance was in love and deep down, she believed and hoped Vera would never come back, and even if she did, it would be heartless and callous of Richmond to throw her out just like that. If such a situation arose, she would not mind being a second wife. Richmond knew he was not in love with Constance. She had simply warmed herself into his life when he needed a companion. In fact, the turn of events as maneuvered by Constance, greatly surprised him. They had lived together without a quarrel for the past five years under one roof. She turned a blind eye to his frivolities and shortcomings and on several occasions, he had been tempted to formalize their relationship, but there was always that fear that she would change her attitude if he married her, and that he would no longer have a hold on her.

Richmond was a nice-natured man. He was quite unfortunate to have had such a horrible childhood and marriage experience but his good nature still came through despite the tough façade he put on. Richy was not selfish and did not ask much of life. What he yearned for most was happiness; the happiness that he was deprived of while growing up. It was this experience that made him vow never to deliberately make anyone unhappy, not even himself.

But Richmond's life was also complicated. Here he was, falling in love with this little school girl, despite all the ups and downs in his life. It must be a joke, he told himself. He had an obsession for decent girls; he found them obedient and easy to manage. He was always careful with the type of girls he picked and he tried to avoid any embarrassing situation, where a parent could sue him for child abuse, neither did he need a young "schoolboy" boyfriend, breaking his windscreen because of some sixteen-year-old beauty; a mere slip of a girl. His specialty was the pretty, decent, quiet and reserved types.

Aima fitted the bill of his ideal woman, but the most disturbing thing about her case was that she was always on his mind, driving him crazy. "Was it her virginity or her naivety that made her so irresistible?" he wondered. She never took special pains to look any different. Her looks were constant; be it first thing in the morning or last thing at night. Her beauty was not as obvious as that of her sister, Inyingi, but it was more alluring.

He could not believe his luck when, after several pleas and visits to Aima's school, she eventually accepted a relationship with him. He could not even believe he was actually pleading with her to be his friend. He knew she liked him, but he could not fathom why she was playing hard-to-get. All the tricks he knew had failed. He was thankful that she had at last conceded to his advances.

He felt it was destiny. On one of the occasions he visited, he was told she was sick and could not come out to the car park to see him. She never allowed him to visit her in the hostel but she always preferred meeting him in his car. He asked if he could see her and was told, he couldn't. He went back the next day and was told the same thing. Out of concern, he asked the porter if he could go into the hostel to see her and was told this was a university, and there were no strict restrictions as regards visitors to female hostels, especially during stipulated visiting hours.

Aima almost collapsed when she saw him. He apologized for the visit and said he had to see her out of concern for her health. She looked pale and sick. He inquired what was wrong and was informed she had malaria and had taken some drugs.

"Are you on a prescription?"

"No," she answered. She had bought the drugs from a chemist.

He immediately asked her to get dressed because he was taking her to the hospital. To his surprise, she obeyed without any objection or hesitation.

They were lucky to have gone to the hospital at the time they did, because she was whisked off to the emergency room as soon as they arrived. Tests were run immediately and it was discovered that Aima had typhoid fever. She had therefore been taking the wrong drugs. In fact, she would not have survived another forty eight hours if they had not gone to the hospital when they did.

Since she was in good hands, they decided there was no need to inform her family. He visited her everyday, till she recovered. One thing led to another, and before they knew it, their relationship had tilted towards the amorous.

Meanwhile, in the hospital, Aima was worried and scared. She did not want the kind of ailment she had as a child to recur. She kept praying to God to take it away and make her whole. Eventually, she got well and was discharged.

As a growing child, Aima had a seasonal ailment which no one could effectively diagnose. Very fresh in her memory was its recurrence one night when she was four years old. Doctors were not sure of what was wrong with her. All kinds of drugs were administered on her but she did not improve making her family, worry for her. Her mum never left her side at bedtime. At night, Aima would suddenly scream in her sleep causing her mother to also wake up, place her right hand on her and shake her, till she woke up.

"What was the matter?" Her mum would ask, wiping sweat from her forehead with a small towel.

"It was a bad dream." She replied with a shiver.

"What exactly was it about?"

"I don't know mum, but it was terrifying." This always caused her mum great anxiety, causing her mind to wander far and wide. What could be wrong? Why did she have the same terrifying dream all the time?

She invited Pastor Okey from Miracle Pentecostal Church for intercession but all he could do was to pray for her and each time he would say: "Just believe Aima, and the bad dream would disappear, never to come back!" "Amen! Her mother would respond.

The pastor told her mum to read the scriptures to Aima in place of bedtime stories. Ibiye grew stronger spiritually because of Aima's illness. Every night, Ibiye would call her children together and read a portion of the Bible to them. Then she would interpret the scriptures as it relates to everyday life. Aima looked forward to these Bible sessions. In fact, she fantasized about the stories told her by her mum. As her mother narrated the stories, she would imagine she was watching a movie. These stories made her appreciate the importance of giving and helping people in need, and she decided to take a cue from this fact of life.

When Aima got tired of the doctor's drugs, she pleaded with her mum to discontinue with the drugs; their smell nauseated her! Her mum, of course, would not hear of it, so Aima developed a ploy. Whenever she could, she avoided taking the drugs. Even when her mum personally dispensed them, she would hide them most of the time to throw away when no one was watching. Of course, she was getting better miraculously.

Eventually, the illness left as it came and no one really knew what the ailment was. Aima used to loose weight and faint when it comes. The dreams, however, continued whenever she was sick. Aima kept wondering why her dreams caused her to scream at night, and why they were always consistent especially whenever she fell ill. The details were always the same. It took her another seven years before she could comprehend the content of the dream. She also realized it occurred only when she has an ailment. "What is the meaning, and why the same dream?" She pondered. Because of the recurrence of the dream, her mum had gotten used to the symptoms. Aima always screamed out in her sleep with her eyes still shut: "No! No! Help! Help!" Then she would wake up.

Over the years, she was able to make out the content of the dream, but she refused to disclose it to anybody because it made no sense to her. When her father came back from the United Kingdom, he observed the incidence a few times and being a medical doctor, tried counseling her and urged her to tell him the details of the dream but she insisted that she could not recollect. She felt it was very annoying for anyone to pry into what she considered her private life. It got to a point that the whole household got weary of it. People offered suggestions and at a point everyone grew curious. They wanted to know what the dream was all about. When she was young, the prayer was that the dream should never recur, but now everybody's prayer was for her to remember what it was so they would know how to tackle the problem.

One day, her brother Dabo asked: "Aima! Are you sure you are telling us the truth? How can you always remember the details of your other dreams but you never remember this one that is constant? I hope you are not hiding anything."

She eyed and ignored him.

"Aima dear, don't mind your stupid brother," advised her mum. "I told you to scream J-E-S-U-S in your dream each time it recurs, why didn't you do that?"

Mum, I tried to but it doesn't seem to come out."

The dream disappeared miraculously when she got into the university. In fact, she did not realize it had disappeared and could not even remember at what particular time it happened. The thought struck her one day when she was with Richmond, sharing a passionate moment.

"Mon beau," her pet name for him, "Have I ever screamed in my sleep?"

"No, never!"

"You mean since we met, you've never heard me scream?"

"No, never. Do you scream in your dreams?" He asked.

But Aima was too excited and seemed lost in thought to answer.

"This is interesting," she said at last.

She got up from the bed she was sharing with him, picked up her dress from a chair by the bed, and hurriedly dressed.

Richmond watched her in amazement.

"Why the hurry?" He asked.

"I must get home. I must see my parents and give them the good news."

"What is so special about your dreams and screams?"

"It's a long story mon beau. Someday, I will tell you all about it, but now I must go and see my parents."

"Cherie, wait. Let's watch the situation for some time. Don't raise your hopes. If it does not recur then you can tell them. But I am very serious. What is so special about all these that you cannot tell me? I'm curious. I love you very much and I believe love is for sharing. I will keep your secret. You know your secrets will be very safe with me. I may even be able to give you some meaningful advice. I'm older and wiser you know?" He stopped for breath and then continued. "You don't have to be too cautious with me. There is nothing about you that can be too bad for me. I will ever remain your beau as long as you would have me, and what I cannot help or change, you have to bear with me."

"What is it that you cannot change?" She asked, as she got to the door.

"You know we can never get married or even have children. But I will show you the kind of love you can never imagine." Replied Richmond.

"Thank you sweetheart. You have solved my puzzle even without knowing what it was about. Our meeting, I believe, was not accidental. It was bound to happen; but how long can we keep up with this relationship? The warning started from when I was four years old."

"Ma Cherie, please stop speaking in parables. You are getting me worried. What have I got to do with your dreams, I did not even know you at that age, or are you asking for some more TLC (tender loving care)?" He questioned jokingly.

Aima failed to see the humour in his remarks but she kept her cool and did not respond. She finally told him to dress up and leave so she could go and see her parents in town. She stood by the exit door and this made him very uneasy. He decided he was not going to approach the topic again until she was willing and ready to talk about it. He got dressed and they left together. All these transpired in the little apartment he had rented for her, off campus.

The apartment was the normal off campus type. He could afford something more sophisticated in a better area of town, even with a chauffeur-driven car, but he decided against it. Everybody knew she was from a modest home and he did not want her to live far above her means. He wanted her to have all the modest comforts she deserved, without attracting too much attention to herself. He also wanted her to pass through the university like any other girl of her age. He loved her very much and wanted her to be happy. In his mind, he did not want to jeopardize her future, by dominating her life, but his actions denote something different.

His reasoning was that, after all, he had lived his life and was even married and has a family. Initially, he had agreed to a relationship bereft of sexual intercourse. She was like an angel that needed to be pampered. But his Adamic nature overtook him and, despite all her initial protests, they went against their agreement and finally made love, one lovely weekend.

CHAPTER 6

The state university has several hostels distributed in estates called Parks for female and male undergraduate students. There are a total of six thousand rooms in the twenty three-storey buildings. There are a total of three Parks: Aba Park, Warri Park and Mandela Park. The post-graduate hostels, made up of six three-storey buildings, were located in Mandela Park. Here, there is an array of other buildings for administration, classrooms, theater, convocation arena and a shopping mall. The university nursery/primary and secondary schools, the University Teaching Hospital as well as a petrol station were all located in Mandela Park. Each of the parks had its own refectory.

The hostels were never enough for the students. In fact, the rooms were allocated on a first-come-first-served basis. There were situations when students who did not have accommodation, paid to share the beds of their luckier colleagues. The living conditions in the hostels were less than satisfactory. There was never any privacy in the rooms or conveniences. Because of these inconveniences, most students preferred renting out-of-campus apartments.

Aima lived in one of such facilities until she decided to avoid Richmond. Each time he asked her out she declined giving one excuse or the other. He never met her in her room anymore. She also refused to reply the notes he dropped on her door. She knew what she ought to do but she couldn't bring herself to do it. She was no longer concentrating on her studies and finally moved into the hostel, to share a bed space with her friend, Ibiene.

Initially, Richmond told himself she must be busy, but with time, it dawned on him that she might actually be avoiding him. Everything seemed to change between them since their discussion on her dreams and screams. He wondered why she had suddenly become estranged from him, especially since she had been genuinely happy when he confirmed to her that she no longer screamed in her sleep. She had even thanked him for solving her puzzle and yet here she was, avoiding him. He wondered what this was all about. What had he to do with the dreams or could it have been a problem she couldn't solve. Worried and concerned, Richmond kept going back to look for her at the apartment he had rented. After several visits, he met a friend of Aima who told him she had moved into the hostel. He got the exact details from the friend and left.

One Thursday, she came back late in the evening; tired and hungry, after spending two or more hours on her course work in the Central Library. Her intention was to get in, eat and sleep.

"Aima!" Ibiene called, just as she stepped into the room. "Guess who was here this evening?"

"Ibiene please spare me stories for now. I am very tired and hungry. I need something to eat." Aima pleaded as she flung her books on the six-inch mattress on the floor at the end of the room.

On a small table, she saw the shopping bag of a popular supermarket in town. Excited, she asked: "Did you go to Excellence after lectures?"

"No, it is for you."

"What do you mean, it is for me?" she queried, picking the bag.

Aima was about to look in the shopping bag, when she suddenly stopped short, like someone held up by an unseen force.

"The visitor dropped this for me?" She asked.

Without waiting for an answer, she dropped the bag, walked back to the door and shut it.

"Richmond was here. He brought that for you." Ibiene explained.

"How did he get my new address?"

"Didn't you tell him you are now staying with me?"

"No!" Aima snapped. Visibly worried, she sat on the mattress.

Ibiene reached out and collected the bag. She brought out a small note and showed it to Aima.

"Well, he said I should give you this note. He looked very worried. I didn't know where to reach you. He waited for more than an hour before leaving. He pleaded that you call him as soon as you are back."

Aima took the note from her and read.

"What's the matter?" asked Ibiene on seeing the grimace on her face. "It appears you don't want him around you any longer?"

Nervous, Aima stood up and walked to the door, then turned and faced her friend.

"Exactly! Ibiene, you can't understand. Richmond is a guy I really love. I would not have wanted the relationship to end but...!"

"Why? I find him lovable and responsible." Ibiene asked surprised.

"You are right. He is lovable and responsible, but the fact remains that Richmond is a married man with children. What does he want from me?" She sat down on the mattress again, thoughtful. She then looked at her friend, "Listen Ibiene, to continue with this relationship would mean embarking on a journey that leads nowhere. I don't see any future in the affair. That is why I have decided to end the relationship and face my studies."

Aima thought of her recurring dream. How long could she keep it a secret? She had not even had the courage to confide in her own sister, Inyingi. Somehow, on this fateful day, she found herself narrating the mysterious dream to Ibiene. She told her the dream was always the same.

"In the dream I was walking on a lonely footpath when suddenly, I got to a bridge. I needed to cross to the other side, but each time I placed a foot on the bridge, it was as if the wooden bridge would give way. This made me scream with fear of falling into the river and under the bridge. To me, there are two possible interpretations to this dream. First, Richmond is the bridge, and everything about him showed the gap between us: the age difference, his marital status, his achievements in life, his circle of friends etc. I feel that my relationship with Richmond will not yield anything positive. That is why the bridge threatened to give way in my dream." She paused and looked worriedly at Ibiene. After a while, she continued.

"Ibiene, listen. I need to write my own story. The answer and realization gave me only two options: it is either I continue the relationship with Richmond and live a false life, which is against my principles or end it straight away. If I continue this relationship, what will be my future? Will it be right?"

"My candid opinion is that you discuss this issue with him before making any rash decisions." A visibly puzzled Ibiene said hesitantly.

Richmond waited for weeks for her call but got none. Frightened and confused he decided to make a final attempt at contacting her. He was even tempted to ask Inyingi for assistance but was not sure of what the outcome would be. To make sure the letter he had written gets to her, he sent it through a courier service.

Incidentally, Aima was in her room when the courier man called.

"Aima?"

Aima looked at him with suspicion.

"Yes. What can I do for you?" She answered sternly staring at the man.

"I have a mail for you," he said.

Aima became silent.

He brought out a dispatch notebook, passed a biro pen to her and showed her where to sign. Aima signed and thanked him. She turned the envelope and read the name on the reverse side… Richmond. She shivered and wondered why he had to send her mails through a courier. Slightly agitated, she tore the envelope as she entered her room, sat on the mattress and began to read:

Ma Cherie,

Why are you avoiding me? What have I done? Please as soon as you receive this letter call me so we can discuss like two mature people. I know you need your 'space'. I will respect that, but please, if we are parting, let us part like friends and not like enemies.

I am patiently waiting to receive your call.

Beau

She passed from sadness to surprise and then confusion. After a long reflection, she felt she owed him some explanations and decided to soften her stance and give him a call. She reasoned that after all, he had taken the initiative to contact her and even proposed they part like friends.

She left the room immediately and made her way to a payphone. As she dialed his number, she felt her heart skipped a beat. When he picked up the phone, she spoke.

"Hello! This is Aima calling."

"Ma Cherie, how are you?" Richmond asked.

"Fine," she said. "I just got your letter and decided to call you immediately."

"I appreciate it!" He paused, and then continued. "Aima, what exactly is happening? You changed accommodation without notifying me. Ma Cherie, you never acknowledged my notes." He paused. There was no response from Aima, so he continued his voice somewhat uncertain... Again he paused, to allow her respond but she was not forthcoming. Now, unable to contain his emotions he called out: "Aima!"

"Yes, I am listening," was her faint answer.

"Have I offended you in anyway? I can apologize. You see, I love you..." Just as he said these words, he heard his live-in lover walk into the bedroom. Richmond became nervous and rushed to end the conversation to avoid a crisis.

"I will see you later Aima," he whispered. "Wait for me at your hostel."

"I can't hear you. Can you speak up?" Aima appealed from the other end.

"I have a sore throat. I will see you tomorrow."

The lady closed the door just as Richmond rushed his parting words and dropped the phone.

"Who was that you were speaking to?" She asked in suspicion.

"Ah! A business associate," replied Richmond, and tried to change the subject. "By the way, I forgot to tell you..."

"A business associate? Then why the hurry to terminate your conversation?" She queried. "And by the way, you never told me you had a sore throat."

Richmond became nervous. To his surprise she got very angry and he attempted to make light of the incidence.

"As a matter of fact, I was joking."

"I think I have had enough," she said. "I don't even know what I am doing with you. Not only have you refused to marry me, now you deny me respect. One of these days, I will leave your house."

With this, she stomped out of the room, swearing and cursing.

Richmond was too angry to respond. He could not understand why she came in just at the time Aima called him.

On her part, Aima was surprised at the sudden sore throat and how abruptly he had ended their conversation. She felt he was up to some pranks and decided not to wait for him the next day.

Though Richmond suspected Aima would not wait for him, he still got up early and set off to find her at the hostel. "If only Aima had a phone, I would call her, but phones are only for the privileged students." He thought. He got dressed, entered his Lexus jeep and headed for her hostel.

"Hi, Aima. I thought I wouldn't meet you at home," he said, nervously wringing his hands.

"Well, I wasn't expecting you today since you said you had a sore throat. So how is the throat?" She asked without letting him into her room.

"I am fine." He glanced at her with a flash of passion in his eyes and then added: "Where do we start?"

"From the sore throat, and the abrupt way you ended our conversation the last time I called."

"I am really sorry about it," he apologized. "My wife came in and I had to cut the line in a hurry."

This statement gave Aima the courage to continue.

"You see the problem I have been avoiding? Intruders always have their lines cut in a hurry."

"How do you mean?"

She narrated her dreams and her interpretation of it and concluded by letting him know she couldn't continue with the relationship.

"You see, there is no future in this venture. I can see only heartaches, bitterness and sorrow ahead. I don't think I will stake my happiness on such a foolhardy adventure and would rather, we say our goodbyes."

"So this is it… this is the end?"

"It is, my love. I don't want to take anymore chances for I have taken enough as it is. I read somewhere that the more chances you take, the fewer there is left.

"My darling, don't you think you are overreacting? Please take some time to reconsider your decision which I think…"

"There is nothing to reconsider. I do love you Eddy but as I said earlier, I can see only darkness ahead. I'm sorry but I have to go. This is the end my love. I wish you the best in your endeavours."

With that she entered her room, shutting the door in his face.

****

Aima decided to spend the next weekend at home. She needed that interval to get over her break-up with Richmond. She bought mangoes on her way because Inyingi loved to eat them.

"What is the secret of your trim look? You eat like a horse, yet you always look slim?" Aima asked her sister.

Three days had gone by since her parting ways with Richmond. She saddened and sorrowed at her loss and had embraced the solace of solitude at her sister's flat. Despite frequent prodding, she refused to disclose the reason for her silence to Inyingi, but today, she decided to live and socialize again. "Why pine for a man that already has a family," she wondered.

"It is the Lord's doing. The Lord knows I dread being fat, that's why He keeps me trim," replied Inyingi, oblivious of her sister's train of thought.

"You'd better watch what you eat, if not, soon you won't look this beautiful and trim and even the Lord would get tired of doing His thing for you!"

They both burst into raucous laughter

"What forms are you filling?" Aima asked after the laughter had subsided.

"It is an application to contest for the Miss Africa Beauty Pageant. I got it from one of their agents," replied Inyingi. "The agent had approached me and asked if I was interested. The prizes were tempting and it did not take long for me to succumb."

Aima went through the forms with Inyingi, filled it and prayed she would scale through the audition. The prizes will come in handy.

"How is Mr. Dateme?" Aima asked. "It is long I heard anything about him from you."

"He is now history," was Inyingi's response.

"What? Why?" Aima asked.

"He is putting pressure on me for marriage, but I am really not ready to settle down now. I don't want to be tied to one man yet."

"Sister Inyingi that is not an excuse. You are not growing any younger; most girls your age are already married and have kids. Don't you ever miss having a family of your own?"

"What about your newfound heartthrob?" Inyingi quibbled, changing the subject.

"Who are you talking about?"

"Richmond, of course! Did you have a quarrel with him?"

"Not at all, but if you don't mind, let's change the subject."

"Has he asked you to marry him?" "Are you no longer interested in him?"

"On the contrary, the answer is 'no' to all your questions. The problem is, he is too good, too nice and I am madly in love with him. But I had to stop because it is morally wrong, and apart from that, we kept on hiding from everybody and everything. He told me we could never get married. He has a political ambition, so he has to do everything right so that his opponents won't pull him down. There is a bridge between us; everything about us is worlds apart."

"Like what?" Inyingi asked.

"Everything… His… Oh! But this bridge…"

"What bridge?" Inyingi asked again.

"You remember when I was a kid, up till the age of adolescence; I used to have recurring nightmares. I actually dreamt about a bridge. Each time I tried to put a foot on the bridge; it shook as if it was going to collapse."

"I see your point," replied Inyingi. "So you are comparing your relationship with Richmond to this bridge? Well it's up to you, but I don't think you should let him go."

****

This particular September was the worst month in Richmond Junior's life. His father took ill and was hospitalized. A call came through from the United States informing him that Vera, his wife, had lost her life in a hurricane. As if that was not enough, Constance moved out of his house because she was tired of waiting for him to ask her hand in marriage. From the look of things, it seemed he would never propose so she decided to give him an ultimatum: he had three months to decide if he wanted to marry her. She was upset because many people came to pay their condolences to him after the death of his wife,

Vera, and nobody seemed to accord her the respect she desired. In fact, she saw nothing but pity for her in the eyes of his visitors.

Constance moved out, out of annoyance and pride. On his part, Richmond was upset with her actions. They were justifiable, he agreed, but he felt the timing was wrong. She had abandoned him at the time he needed her most. Inyingi and some of her sibling also came to sympathize with him, but Aima did not. Inyingi informed him even without being asked that Aima had gone for the National Youth Service Corps (NYSC), in Lagos at the completion of her course work and graduation. Family members intervened in the situation between him and Constance. They tried to convince him to marry her but he was adamant in his resolve not to forgive her. He was actually too upset to consider the issue of marriage. He missed her kids whom he had gotten used to like his own, but that was not enough for him to go and look for her.

CHAPTER 7

It was 6 am on a wet morning in April. Rain was still falling when Ibiye went into Dabo's room and met him still asleep. Furiously, she called out: "Dabo, wake up! You lazy man, when are you going to move into your own apartment? You have been working for the past three years. All you do is work, go to parties and sleep. Do you save money at all for the future?"

The Richardsons now lived in their own house, after spending five years in the four-bedroom flat provided by the hospital. Frank had bought a vast hectare of land in which he had built his dream home. The house had a very high brick fence and a massive gate. The gatehouse was on the right hand of the entrance, inside the compound. The left side has no obstruction and led to their modest six-bedroom bungalow. By the right of the building, were different trees, bearing choice fruits – guava, pawpaw, mango, coconut and pink apples. Farther right is the garage housing a fairly used Toyota Tercel car.

Behind the main house is a two-room boy's quarter, which Dabo converted to a chalet. The house sat on a beautiful landscape, surrounded by flowers. Ibiye's favourite was the queen of the night because of its exotic fragrance. Most nights, she ate her dinner on the terrace while waiting for her husband to get back from work.

Dabo, refused to move out of his parent's house. He was not married and so did not see any reason to move to a rented apartment. After all, he was comfortable and independent on his father's premises.

His life was regimented. From Monday to Friday, he got up in the morning, had breakfast in the main house then went off to work. He would return at 5 pm, have an early dinner in the main house and then retire to his abode. Once in a while, he brought home a female companion. While his guest remained in his chalet, he would collect food from the main house for her.

Friday nights were his outing nights. He would leave the house by 9 pm and return in the early hours of the morning. On Saturdays, he attended functions like weddings, birthday parties, workshops, seminars or whatever activities he was invited to. For his outings, he borrowed his father's car whenever it was available. On any free day, he stayed indoors or visited Inyingi and Aima. He never went to church and Ibiye, his mother, had gotten tired of inviting him

*   *   *   *   *

Petromina worked in Ashama Nightclub in Port Harcourt. She always left her house early in the evening and returned at dawn, the following day. On this particular day, she left her house a little earlier with the intention of buying a few items at the mall close to her office. Island Shopping Mall had a wide variety of shops, partitioned with glass while some shops were in the halls. Petromina and her friends used to tease that the owners of the corridor shops avoided having to pay rent like the owners of the main shops. It was always easier for her to pick up a few items from the corridor shops on her way to work and then cross over to the nightclub, through the side entrance of the mall.

One day, as she walked in through the main entrance, she caught sight of a roughly-dressed young man. She even smiled at him for she thought she knew him. He looked like one of the bouncers in the nightclub where she worked. He was still within her sights as she walked through some shops at the mall. But this time, she noticed that he was with a young, elegantly dressed lady. His companion was dark in complexion, and had on a red spaghetti-strapped chiffon dress. She was sure this lady had passed by her earlier, but she had not taken particular notice of her.

She concluded her shopping and headed for the till to pay. She dipped her hand into her bag but to her surprise, her purse was gone. In its place was a note that read: "Read. We are watching U."

Petromina looked up. The couple nodded and smiled at her. With trembling fingers, she opened the note and began to read:

Don't try to be smart, we are watching you. There is a parcel in your bag. Take it with you to work. Early in the morning, before you close from your work, you will see a young man in a wine-coloured shirt, sitting at the right hand of the entrance to the club, on the last row of tables. Go to him and be nice to him. Offer to pay for his drinks with the enclosed cash. And wink your right eyelid twice.

If he is the right person, he would respond by winking back. When you have ascertained he is the person, ask him for a ride home in his car. Give the parcel to him in the car and collect our cash of N5,000 from him. He is aware of the amount. We will come and pick it from your house in the afternoon.

If he fails to show up, take the parcel home. As soon as you finish reading, tear this note and drop it at the spot you are standing.

We are still watching you.

Petromina was jittery on her way to work. In fact, she was scared. She did not know what she had gotten herself into. She looked round; the man and the woman seemed to have disappeared but she knew they had not. She thought she knew who they wanted her to deliver the parcel to. She was surprised that her contact person was that irresponsible. She had heard that his father was a medical doctor and that he had a good job. Why then was he doing drugs? Anyway, it was not her place to speculate. She just wanted to be done with this obnoxious assignment, quit this job and even move from her house. Why did they pick on her? What will happen in the end? Would they kill her?

*   *   *   *

At Ashama Nightclub, Eric sat quietly observing Petromina as she made her blunders on the night of the incidence. Eric was in the team that recruits new members. They had intended recruiting an additional hand and Petromina would have been employed had she passed her test. Unknown to her, TBK Marketing Department had been on her trail for some time. They had spent three months investigating her background. She was one of six names they had short listed for this job. Out of the six, only one person passed the test and was recruited.

For three months, TBK watched her every movement; from the time she left the house till she returned at night. They also monitored her to her village when she visited her folks. From investigations, they reckoned she was a good candidate but the final test would determine whether to approach her for the job or not. She would pass if she promptly delivered the parcel to the correct person and did not abscond from her home or workplace out of fear. If she chickened out, she would fail the test without ever knowing she was being tested for a job.

Due to the nature of its underground work, the company could not advertise in the open market for vacancies in this department. They looked for people who were desperately in need of cash and were willing to do anything, except kill, for money. The person recruited also needed to be able to appear innocent after the assignment had been carried out. Mr. Terrence strictly advised against any form of bloodshed.

For the past three months, Fredrick and an assigned member of staff watched Petromina. They noticed that despite her job at the nightclub, she did not have many friends. A few people, mainly men, hung around with her. This was a good sign because they reasoned that girls are talkative. If she had female friends, she might be tempted to discuss her job with them should she be eventually employed.

They also watched her travel to the village every fortnight. Their trail to her village took them to a remote hut, somewhere in Isiala Ngwa Local Government Area in the eastern region of Nigeria. On further investigations, it was discovered that she was an osu. Osus were outcasts or the untouchables. The story went that in the days gone by, men were sacrificed to the gods of their land. The families of the victims then became known as the osus. It was believed that any association with them could bring bad luck. They were therefore not allowed to inter-marry with non-osus or even co-habit with them. In most villages in the east where this practice exists, osus are given land, far away from the other indigenes.

Petromina's family lived in a thatched hut, in the outskirts of the village. As a kid, she would trek a long distance before she got to school. Nobody played with her in school. When she and her siblings go to the stream to fetch water, everybody stood aside, away from them until they filled their water pots and left. They grew up with this discrimination and accepted it as their fate. After her secondary school education, Petromina was admitted into the University of Port Harcourt. She could however not attend the school because she couldn't afford the fees. The opening otherwise afforded her the opportunity to visit Port Harcourt. After a vigorous job hunt, she got eventually got employed at the nightclub.

Surprisingly, nobody knew anything about osus here. Her ambition was to work hard and bring out her family from the bush. Every fortnight, she traveled to her village to spend time with her family.

On this fateful night, she kept making mistakes at the club. After she had spilled drinks twice, the supervisor asked her if she was okay; she answered in the affirmative. She was so preoccupied with her thoughts that she did not know when Dabo came in. she was so sure that the parcel was for Dabo that she did not bother to check the colour of his shirt. She went straight to him, reminding herself that she had been told to be nice to him.

"Hi handsome," she winked twice.

"Hello pretty," he responded with a wink.

"Can I pay for your drinks?" She asked.

"Who am I to refuse a pretty damsel? What is the catch?" He asked.

"Just a free ride home," she responded.

"I am game."

By this he meant that it was okay by him.

"Are you alone tonight?" She asked.

"Yes, waiting for you," he replied.

Dabo actually played along because Ashama Nightclub was one of his favourite clubs. The waitresses were pretty and smart. In fact, he was told most of them were decent and responsible girls. He was therefore surprised when Petromina started flirting with him. Despite the fact that she was always officious, she was one of his favourites. He always enjoyed chatting with her but today she came to him willingly. He was not going to pass up this opportunity. He waited until she closed from work and entered his borrowed car.

"My name is Dabo, what is yours?"

"I already know you," she said. "You are a regular clubber here. My name is Petromina, Pet for short."

"That is a lovely name," he remarked.

They kept up their conversation as he drove to her house when he suddenly stopped and parked the car by the side of the road because of engine problem.

"Here is the parcel. Can I have the money?" Petromina asked, thinking he was acting according to plan.

"What parcel?" He asked, dismayed.

"I was told you knew about it," she said, passing the parcel to him. "Here it is. Take it and give me the five thousand naira."

Dabo was confused. Nothing made sense anymore. He decided to check what it contained.

"I don't think it is necessary to check. I was told you would just give me the money."

As they were still arguing, a police patrol car pulled up by their side and before they could hide the parcel, the policemen saw it and checked to see what it was. Dabo and Petromina were arrested and taken to the police station.

In the station, Dabo sneaked a note to his parents through a police officer that had just completed his night shift. Petromina had nobody to call; her family was in the village. She was the breadwinner of her family and had come to Port Harcourt to make money and assist with the upkeep of those in the village.

****

TBK Nigeria Limited was an interior decorating firm. On the surface they specialized in the decoration of houses, residences, offices, hotels and schools. The staffers were always well-dressed, courteous, prim and proper. Nothing in their outward appearance showed the type of underground deals they were involved in.

They also sold and supplied household furniture, some of which were imported and the others, locally manufactured. Their motto was: 'excellence'. They were always smart and careful. Their services were superb, thanks to the caliber of staff they employed and the training they gave. But underground, they were involved in the sale of narcotics as well as the practice of prostitution.

The company had several departments. The Managing Director/CEO, Tekena Terrence, personally supervised the marketing aspect of the underground deals.

One of the other departments was manufacturing. The General Manager, Mr. Fredrick was in charge of recruiting staffers for manufacturing and sales. While he put out his vacancy notices in the other departments for purpose of employment, the marketing arm engaged its members of staff by more subtle and creative means, avoiding publicity by all means.

The members of staff in the manufacturing sector and those in the front desk were only aware of what their jobs entailed. They were blissfully ignorant of the dark side of the firm.

The marketers were always well turned out, looking good. This applied to both the males and the females. They had the privilege of traveling far and wide to bring in clients and businesses. The marketers' functions included: escort, prostitution, courier and sale of Indian hemp, cocaine or any available hard drug. Sometimes, they had to carry out other functions that were assigned to them.

These special squads were recruited on the recommendations of people in the business. Sometimes, Mr. Fredrick had to come up with ways to recruit people on his own. Thos who do not apply willingly were assessed on the job, while they were placed on probation. Fredrick looked out for decent, smart-looking young men and women, who were desperate for cash. Different people were interviewed in different ways.

For now, the company needed more hands in the marketing sector. Hands were needed to fill in the gaps created by the exit of three of the key staff who had recently gotten married and had been paid off.

******

Dr. Richardson arrived at the police station that Saturday afternoon looking worried and confused. He had been told nothing could be done to effect the release of Dabo till the following Monday. Dabo swore his innocence to his father. His only offence was to give a ride to a pretty lady in his car. He even argued that if the substance was his, the police would not have caught them arguing. He would have simply accepted it, paid and dropped her off.

Monday came and the story became different. Dr. Richardson was told he still could not bail Dabo since any drug-related case in the country was not treated with levity. He was told the case would be taken to court and that Dabo would remain in police custody till a date was fixed for the hearing.

Meanwhile, Petromina was confused. She now had a double mind; could it be that she had made a mistake or was she conned into it? She had been told the recipient would not argue but she could remember the astonished look on Dabo's face when he opened the parcel. She realized too late that she had made a mistake for the parcel was not for Dabo. She felt sorry that she had gotten him into this mess. When they took them to the police station, she had called a senior female police officer to a corner of the hall to try and convince her that she had made a mistake. She told her that Dabo was innocent but the officer simply looked at her with disgust and asked her to keep quiet. When Dabo's parents accosted her, she also narrated all that had happened, emphasizing the innocence of their son. They were happy knowing Dabo had a good case.

CHAPTER 8

Richmond Jnr. was in a state of confusion. His world seemed to be collapsing around him. His father's health was fast deteriorating but it seemed to have brought them closer. He prayed for his recovery for he still needed him around to run the affairs of the hotel. He wanted to try his hands at politics. In fact, he had been approached on the subject by friends in different parties. In one party, a friend was offering him the position of Deputy Governor while in another he was asked to represent his constituency in the House of Assembly. He decided to ignore his marital problems, hide his feelings and continue his day-to-day transactions. He started to devote more time to his sons; not only did he hire a nanny; he also got personally involved in their welfare. Above all, he stopped chasing after women.

One day, as he was listening to the network news at 9 pm, an advert came up during the commercial break that caught his attention. It was about a certain preacher who was coming to Port Harcourt to preach on a particular day at the Presidential Hotel. The preacher invited those who were burdened to come and feel the touch of God. Although Richmond Jnr. was not a believer, he decided to attend, though his reasons were not quite clear even to himself. It was certainly not for salvation. As an aspiring politician, he tried to attend as many functions as possible and at each occasion, ensured he made maximum impact. Another reason he decided to attend the programme was to make friends for his political benefit.

At the crusade, he answered an invitation by the preacher to all non-believers to surrender their lives to Christ. This he did simply by believing that Jesus was the Son of God and Saviour of the world. He decided to hand over his life to Christ that day.

Surprisingly, before the event was over, Richmond was touched by the Holy Spirit. He experienced a sense of joy and peace in his spirit with this decision. He sang all the way as he drove home. At home, his kids were surprised to see their father, laughing and singing.

A few weeks later, things started changing for the better. His father miraculously recovered. He joined the Democracy for All Party (DAP), as the Deputy Governorship candidate. He also seemed to be smiling more these days. As if that was not enough, one day as he was having lunch at his office, his father sent a messenger to call him. He dreaded any session with his father because he would spend much time with him and so took his time before going to see him.

When he came to his father's office, he greeted a woman sitting on the visitors' seat and headed straight for the couch.

"Junior, come over here," called his father.

Richmond Jnr. Had hoped that his father would join him on the couch to discuss whatever it was he had invited him for. He hesitated, walked up to the table and took the vacant seat close to the lady. He observed that the lady looked familiar, but he kept this to himself and sat quietly beside her.

"Woman, could you repeat your story," requested his father.

The lady turned her eyes on Richmond Jnr. hesitated for a while, and began:

"Junior, my son," she said, "I am your mother."

Eddy looked at his father who shrugged his shoulders as if to isolate himself from what the woman had just said.

"I am sorry for all the sorrow and pains I might have caused you. When I was pregnant, my doctor told me I had a terminal disease and that I might not even carry the pregnancy to term. I pleaded with him to do everything possible to save the life of my baby..." she hesitated and then as if delighted she was revealing a secret, burst out, "You are my baby."

She stopped and looked tenderly at Eddy for a while. Both men had listened without interrupting her. She continued with renewed vigor: "I did not inform my husband. Besides, I swore the doctor to secrecy. I was quite certain my husband would want to do his best to save my life and in the end, I would still die. I didn't want to prolong his agony and anxiety. The doctor agreed to inform my family members of my death after the delivery. I wanted members of my family to feel the pain only once."

She noticed some uneasiness in Eddy, who turned and questioned his father: "But dad, did they not bury my mother's corpse?"

"No," answered his father. "You see, the doctor told us she knew she was going to die and so signed a note authorizing the hospital to bury her. Her reason was that she wanted everybody that knew her to remember her the way she lived her life and not as she looked in death. That was exactly how it happened. As a matter of fact, I was in such agony that I couldn't think properly."

Again, the woman turned and looked tenderly at her son. Eddy shook his head sideways in utter disbelief.

"But dad, it was irresponsible."

"I never believed a doctor could tell such an expensive lie."

"Please no one should blame the doctor, the woman interrupted. "He was very uncomfortable with the arrangement though he finally obliged me after I had begged him fervently."

The men became quite uneasy. The senior got up and began pacing the room, his hands behind his back.

"So, where have you been all these years?" Her son nervously questioned.

"Benin Republic, my dear." She responded. "My doctor in Nigeria had referred me to a specialist hospital in Benin Republic. There was a new drug they were trying out on people with such an ailment as mine. I was on of the volunteers for the experiment and was fortunate it worked."

Her son shrugged his shoulders, stood by her and looked right into her eyes with a stern expression.

"Why didn't you come back all these years?"
She gazed at him for a while without blinking. Tears welled up in her eyes but did not drop to the ground. She was visibly pained by the interrogations. She turned her face in the opposite direction and continued her story.

"Several times, I had contemplated coming back home but was at a loss as to where to start from. I learnt that my husband had remarried and that my son had marital challenges. I didn't want to add to your burden. Then one day, someone informed me that my husband was sick. That was why I damned all the consequences and retuned."
She suddenly stopped, turned and looked at both father and son, imploring them with her eyes to understand.
Her husband, who was at a loss of what to say muttered: "So, you... you came to see me dead? Is that not the fact?"

"No! No! Believe me," she struggled to explain. "I just realized how hard and hurtful it had been without you people all these years."

"So what is your next plan?" They asked in unison.

"I will spend a few days here," she explained. "Thereafter, I'll go back to Benin

Republic. I have an established business there. I have not remarried."

The tears now began to drip. She got up and wiped her eyes with a handkerchief. She blew her nose silently into it and wiped off the running catarrh.

Eddy looked on completely unexcited. The woman who was before him claiming to be his mother was like a stranger to him. He felt no bond towards her after those wasted and unhappy years he had lived without the care, warmth and love of a mother.

His mother looked at him, anguish wrenching her heart. Then in a tremulous voice, she sobbed out: "Junior, I hope you will forgive me?"

Eddy looked her for a while, his own eyes beginning to well up.

"I have forgiven you," he said, stifling the urge to weep. He dipped his hands in his trousers pocket, collected a handkerchief and wiped his eyes.

Encouraged by a flicker of change on his countenance, she opened her arms to him for an embrace. Her husband watched as Eddy and his mother embraced for the first time. She was like a stranger to him though and he never felt any bond towards her. Both men forgave her.

She went back home with Eddy Jnr. and met her grandsons for the first time. Both mother and son had many questions to answer from the kids. One of the twins asked their father if he had just bought a mummy for himself! The other went on to plead with his father to buy them a new mummy too.

CHAPTER 9

Aima completed her NYSC successfully in Lagos and was employed by an oil company, Elf Nigeria Limited. She was lucky because her hometown was in the oil-rich Niger Delta region of Rivers State, Nigeria. Each year, the oil companies in the country reserve a quota for the employment of indigenes from the Niger Delta and Aima was fortunate to be one of the beneficiaries of this scheme.

After one year of working, the company sent her to the head office in France. Whilst there, she learnt the French language, made friends and lived a very comfortable life. Financially, things looked good but her emotional life was a different story. The last time she called home, all she heard was bad news. For several months, Dabo had been in police custody awaiting trial for a case he swore he was innocent of. Inyingi had contracted a mysterious illness of which doctors could do nothing to save her. She died. Her parents told her the illness was as a result of a sexually transmitted disease. They told her not to bother to attend her funeral as they are burying her expeditiously due to time and social constraints. In Africa, whenever someone dies of a sexually transmitted disease, it always leaves a stigma on the bereaved family. Her parents also informed her that there would be a memorial seminar in the fifth year of Inyingi's death. She planned to visit them then. She had even informed them she might take Moty with her back to France. For several weeks, Aima lost appetite for food as well as the zeal to socialize as she grappled with the realization that her beloved sister has joined the majority.

For about two years now, Aima had been going out with a young Frenchman, Monsieur Pierre Durand. What she felt for him was certainly not love; he just happened to be the best among the lot she had encountered in recent times. Pierre was very understanding and nice to her.

******

Meanwhile, there was tension in TBK Nigeria Limited. Fredrick felt he had overestimated Petromina's intelligence. They had watched silently for several months but the case had still not gone to court. Fredrick was not sure if

Petromina recognized him and if she could give the police a good description of him. He was not prepared for the publicity that would follow such an exposure. Until now, they had always carried out their business without attracting attention. They had several high-network customers, whom the company needed to protect. He was even tempted to go against the company's policy by arranging Petromina's death in detention but decided against it. Terrence had called him in and instructed that he do everything within his reach to protect the name of the company from any form of scandal. Mr. Terrence was a well-respected man in the society; it would be very embarrassing for the other side of him to be discovered.

The case was finally taken to court. A lawyer was assigned to Petromina by the government while the Richmond family got a defense attorney for Dabo.

In court, Petromina insisted she did not know the man that gave her the substance. She said she did not even know what the substance was and how it got into her bag. All she saw was a note and an instruction, which she obeyed for fear of punitive consequences. Dabo's lawyer asked her what gave her the impression the parcel was for Dabo and she replied that where he usually sat at the club suited the description in the note. She was asked if the table was numbered and she replied in the negative, but insisted that it was at a corner and towards the end of the hall. The lawyer told her to repeat the instruction in the note as best as she could recollect and she tried to remember the exact text:

...you will see a young man sitting on the last row at the right hand side of the club. You are to be nice to him. Pay for his drinks, and ask for a ride in his car...

"That was the exact text," she asserted.

"Interesting!" The lawyer exclaimed. "Miss Petromina," he continued, "How interesting that you are able to remember the exact text of the note!"

"I remembered the words because I read the note repeatedly.

The lawyer considered her for a while and then asked: "Is there any other thing you have remembered?"

"Yes. The right person was supposed to be expecting the parcel and he knew the exact amount to be handed over."

"Did the note describe the person or what he was to wear?"

"Yes, a wine coloured shirt, but there was no description of the person." She replied nervously.

For the first time, it struck her that she had missed a very important detail. Although the colour of the shirt Dabo wore that night was black it was still tendered as an exhibit.

"Can you recognize the shirt?" The lawyer asked.

"Certainly, it was the shirt Dabo wore that night."

"What was Dabo's reaction when you handed the parcel to him?"

"He was surprised," she responded.

At this point, Dabo's lawyer gave his closing statement, citing the testimony of the other defendant as proof of his client's innocence. He further urged the court to free his client unconditionally and without delay as his continued detention and trial was a travesty of justice, one which the nation is trying hard to correct in this period of national rebirth.

The prosecutor however argued that Dabo was a chameleon. He drew the judge's attention to Dabo's early lifestyle and how he had been in a remand home because of his wayward acts.

At the end of the case, Dabo was discharged and acquitted.

Fredrick was in court. He was happy that Petromina had not implicated him. He knew she was telling lies; she actually had a good description of him and wondered why she had lied. He was not worried for what they had given her was actually talc powder. It was just a test. It was only a recruited member they gave hard drugs to deliver. Even if she had described him to them and he had been caught, he would simply had apologized and told them it was meant to be a joke. He decided he would assist in getting Petromina off the hook although she had failed the initial test, by not taking into consideration, every detail in the note. Eric had worn a wine-coloured shirt and had sat behind Dabo in the bar on the night of the incident, yet she had not noticed him. "Maybe, she had a special interest in Dabo," he reasoned.

True to his conviction, Fredrick traveled to Aba from Port Harcourt to mail a letter to Petromina's lawyer, who resided in that city. He did this because he did not want the letter traced to him.

The lawyer received the letter the next day. It read in part:

...the content of the envelope Petromina was carrying was not a narcotic drug. It was a facial talcum powder. Ask for the evidence to be tested in court. This note is not a joke. Take the hint seriously.

At first the lawyer dropped the note in the trash can. There was no way somebody would be locked up for being in possession of ordinary talcum powder. He dismissed the 'joke' and continued with what he was doing.

****

Aima buried all her sorrows in her work. She worked as if there was no tomorrow. She was in a foreign land, cold and alone. She was supposed to be happy yet she was not. Even Pierre's presence had started to irritate her. Nobody in the office suspected what she was going through. They all admired her zeal for work; she excelled in the workplace and was always rated 'A' by her boss.
"Bonjour Mademoiselle," Pierre greeted.
"Good morning to you, Pierre." She returned.
"Aujourd'hui, c'est Ventredi."
"Je le sais, Pierre, I know today is Friday. How can I help you?"
"Aima, have you forgotten the invitation to the Club Dix-Huit?"

"No, Pierre."

"Then hurry up so we don't arrive late."

"I am not feeling too well, Pierre. I think I have malaria."

"Malaria, in Paris?"

"I don't know. I am not sure."

"Have you seen a doctor?"

"In Africa we are all doctors. We only visit the hospital when we can no longer manage the situation. I have had self-medication; Chloroquin, B-complex and some multivitamins," she replied. "Take me home; I would love to cook dinner for you. We will pass off tonight's function and we can attend tomorrow. I should be much better by then."

"Okay," he consented.

When they got home, Pierre watched her prepare a meal of rice, fried plantain and chicken stew. He was amazed at her ease and measuring skill. He watched her simply pour the vegetable oil straight from the can into the hot pot; drop a pinch of salt into the pot, pour a tin of tomato puree into the hot oil and add other ingredients like sliced fresh tomatoes, ground pepper, chicken stock, water and spices, all without any measuring tool. She also didn't measure the rice. After the cooking was done, she served him a large helping and waited for his comments.

"Comme c'est bien delicieux!" He cooed affectionately. "You are such an excellent cook."

"Tu me flatte, Pierre."

"Pas du tout!"

"Merci!" As she stifled a smile of satisfaction. Pierre had another helping.

"Tell me, how did you know the exact quantity of ingredients for different dishes?"

Aima laughed. "The measurements are in my brain," she explained. "Back home in Africa, experience plays the major role. We can measure with our eyes. The only measuring instrument we use is the cooking spoon. The rest, we measure with our eyes and fingers.

Pierre passed the night in her apartment. Although it wasn't in her original plan, she didn't object and was rewarded by crude jokes from her boyfriend. It was a welcome departure from her melancholy. Aima laughed much before falling asleep in his arms on the sitting room couch.

As usual, whenever she fell ill, she dreamt. This time the dream was very different. In her dream, she saw a retarded child that was supposedly hers, but which she had abandoned and gone off to France. And since she got to France, she had not had any contact with the child due to her hectic work schedule for she always left home in the early hours of the morning and returned late at night. This scene suddenly faded, giving way to another. This time the baby had been replaced by a pet puppy, which she took to church. As she stepped into the church, the interior changed to her childhood residence in Abonnema. In their house in the village, she discovered some treasures and helped herself to some. Then her late sister, Inyingi appeared, looking rather healthy. This aspect scared her. Then in another part of the house, there was a party and the people seemed to be enjoying themselves. She looked at herself and felt she was too scantily dressed. As she wondered why she was so dressed, her phone rang and she woke up, thanking God that it was after all a dream.

Aima realized she had actually slept off topless on her couch in Pierre's arms. She picked up the phone and heard her mother's excited voice at the other end of the line announcing that Dabo had been acquitted of all charges, and that he was now a free man. For once in a long while, Aima was genuinely happy.

CHAPTER 10

Petromina's lawyer disregarded the note he had received in the post as he was suspicious of its source. He was not ready to make a fool of himself in court. Petromina herself had told him she was not sure what the substance was but that she suspected it to be cocaine. He risked ridiculing himself if he told them it was talcum powder. He crushed the note, pleaded guilty to the charge of possession of a hard drug and asked the judge to be lenient in his judgment since she was a first offender and the drug had been forced on her by an unknown person. He accepted she was partly to be blamed for keeping her handbag carelessly thus enabling someone to plant the substance in it.

She was sentenced to ten years in prison with hard labour. Petromina was shocked and dumbfounded but her lawyer told her it was the best he could do in the circumstance; her offence was actually punishable by death.

Fredrick was always in court and she always saw him, but out of fear she never gave any indication that she knew him. He felt it was out of loyalty she hadn't told on him and dispatched another letter, this time, to Dabo. It read:

Please help Petromina. She is innocent. I had earlier sent a copy of the attached note to her lawyer but he did not make any use of the information in it to plead her case...

Dabo's first impression after reading through the note was to have nothing to do with Petromina and the people behind her. He decided to treat it as trash and ignore anything it contained. But for each of the four weeks that followed, he received identical notes from the same source. He got worried and showed the note to his parents, who in turn went to their lawyer for advice.

On the scheduled day of meeting, the lawyer was busy but sent his female partner, Mrs. Soso Lime-Juice, to represent him. After going through the letters and hearing from the Richardsons, she told them not to worry. "Whoever is sending the notes is obviously desperate for Petromina's release. They are not after Dabo," she reasoned.

"Listen, I am going to handle the case free of charge. I don't like to see an innocent girl rot in jail, just because there is no one to assist her."

This offer came as a relief to them and the Richardsons expressed their gratitude. Mrs. Soso Lime-Juice took over the case file and after studying it, filed an appeal.

****

Petromina's parents had become worried when she did not visit for a while and the family feared the worst. Mary, her younger sister was sent to Port Harcourt to find out why she had abandoned them. On arrival, Mary found Petromina's house, locked. She sat outside for a while before a neighbour told her the little she knew about the situation. Unfortunately, nobody knew the particular jail Petromina was kept. She then went to Petromina's workplace were the story of her conviction for a drug-related offence and subsequent imprisonment was confirmed. No one knew the exact details so the girl went back home to her parents with the bad news.

Petromina's parents were disturbed with the news. Even though they are poor and has no one to fight for their daughter, they knew the God they served would not abandon them in their time of need.

"Whoever is with the Lord is in majority." "Train up your child in the way he should go, and when he is…" She quoted from scripture.

Pet's mum, though not literate, is vastly versed in scriptures. Each month, she took days off to fast and pray for her daughter. She reminded the Lord of all His promises in the Bible, and prayed He does not desert them. He cannot allow their ray of hope to languish in jail. She had done her part in training her child properly; she knew He will do His also.

After about six months in prison, Petromina was allowed to receive visitors. First, were the female lawyer and different female activist groups and then Fredrick. The latter told her he came in peace. Knowing the officials might be listening, he feigned to be a long-lost friend and told her he owed her some apology and explanations but it would wait till she got out of jail.

The lawyer, Mrs. Soso-Limejuice's ground for appeal was that Petromina was not well represented and a date was fixed for hearing. In court, she contested Petromina's supposed possession of a hard drug. She argued that Petromina was not aware of what she was carrying; she was only doing the work of a courier. She therefore demanded the production in court, of the presumed substance that was found in her possession.

The matter was expeditiously tried and after three hours of legal battle between counsels, the case was adjourned by the trial judge at the instance of the prosecution to enable it produce the substance in question.

On the adjourned date, the exhibit was tendered in court. After preliminary objections by the prosecuting counsel, the exhibited substance was confirmed to be facial talcum powder. After due deliberations, the appeal succeeded and Petromina was discharged and acquitted.

Outside the court, Fredrick was at hand waiting.

"Petromina, let me take you home."

"Do you know him?" Questioned her lawyer.

"Yes, I know him." Replied Petromina.

"Will you then like to join him in his car?"

"No," she answered, with an emphatic shaking of the head.

Fredrick was disappointed and left her with her lawyer who later arranged for her transportation to the village where she was reunited with her family.

******

Meanwhile in Paris, Aima started changing for the better. The news of Dabo' release from detention brought her some much needed succour. She invited him over to France on vacation and he readily accepted the invitation. The whole family agreed that he needed a change of scene. Through the help of her office in France, it was a simple matter securing him a visa.

Dabo arrived at Charles de Gaulle Airport in Paris on a bright summer morning. He could not believe his eyes at what he saw. He thought he was in heaven. The airport seemed to him like outer space. In fact he felt like he was walking on air. "Good heavens! This is beautiful indeed!"

From the terminal, he walked through a long corridor to the arrival hall and from there, followed a monitor screen for directions, which by the way, looked like a television set. Dabo was mesmerized for he had never seen anything like this before. He saw a young French woman and asked: "Please, where do I get my luggage?"

The girl stopped and replied: "Moi, je ne parle pass Anglais. Je suis desolee." Pointing at the screen, she turned and left.

Dabo smiled and joined the traffic of passengers. He found himself at an escalator but did not know what to do next. Luckily, there were regular steps by the escalator and he opted for them. Then he noticed the long queue for customs and immigration, but to his relief the officers spoke English. After stamping his travel documents, one of them gave him directions to the arrival hall. There, he met his sister waiting with a Frenchman. He rushed into her arms, hugged her and shook hands with her companion.

"Mie tubo?" He asked. "Who is this man?"

"I kia bo, my friend," she replied.
She then made the introductions.

"Dabo, please meet my friend, Pierre. He's French. Pierre, this is my brother, Dabo, I have been telling you about."

"How do you do?"

"How do you do too?" Dabo answered.

"What language did you speak with him?" Pierre asked Aima.

"Kalabari. That's the language we speak at Abonnema, my hometown." She explained.

"Bon! Bon!" Responded Pierre.

"But from now on, it would be English. She said, looking at Pierre. "And how was your trip?" She asked Dabo with a smile.

"Fine," he replied. "Paris is really a beautiful city."

A young lady mistakenly bumped into Dabo and dropped her hand luggage, spilling its contents. Muttering her apologies, she went down on her knees, carefully gathered and replaced them in her suitcase and then straightened and walked away still apologetic but totally oblivious of the stares, smirks and giggles from people around.

Dabo, disconcerted, collected his luggage and they all drove to Aima's house with Pierre at the wheel.

Aima and her friends took Dabo out every weekend. He saw the Eiffel Tower and other beautiful places. Every other person looked funny to Dabo. They wore scanty clothes, indicating the heat they felt, while Dabo was freezing. He thought that back home in Africa, women would not be caught – not even at home – in such indecent apparel! Such clothes would certainly be considered as too revealing. Each time Dabo cautioned Aima to dress properly, she would reply: "When in Rome, do as the Romans do." She accused him of being a JJC (Johnny Just Come), who would soon adjust to his new environment. On his part, Dabo wore casuals like singlet, T-shirts, sweatshirts and jackets. Aima used to ask him what he would wear during winter. "Maybe, he will wrap a quilt around his body." She chuckled.

One Saturday as they went out to have lunch at L'Hotel Mireille- a five star hotel, someone walked up to them screaming: "It is a lie! It is a lie! Am I dreaming?"

"No! Odessa, you are not dreaming." Dabo replied as he recognized him.

"What brought you all here?" Odessa asked.

Dabo without answering pointed at Aima, implying that he came to see her.

"I live here," Aima informed him.

"Since when?" Odessa asked, curious.

Without waiting for an answer, he asked for her address and she dictated it to him taking his in return.

"Since I arrived here in France I have avoided Nigerians. I never attend their functions or socialize with them. I mingle only with my colleagues." She told her brother as Odessa left.

"But Odessa is our cousin, and I do remember that dad gave you his numbers and address. Why didn't you give him a call on arrival?"

She smiled at Dabo's questions and continued to explain: "You know how Odessa was back at home. Remember the troubles he used to get you into. He had always been a bad boy and I cannot be too sure he has changed."

Dabo told her he believed Odessa is now matured and had changed for the better.

Odessa visited them the following weekend carrying an overnight bag. Dabo was very happy to see him but Aima wasn't and just ignored him. She would have told Odessa not to come and sleep over without discussing it with her first but she remembered her origins.

Odessa was actually their first cousin. In Africa, cousins are like siblings. In Kalabari culture, Odessa was as good as a brother. He, therefore, did not need her permission to visit or sleep over. These were the very things she had tried to avoid by keeping away from Nigerians. Odessa's father, Adams, was Frank Richardson's elder brother. Odessa's education had ended at the secondary school level for he kept getting into trouble and disgracing the family name. Tired of his lifestyle that sometimes bordered on the macabre, his parents finally sent him to live with an uncle in America. But even in America, he was always in and out of jail.

No one knew how he got to France since there was no family member living with him here. No one knew whether he had changed for the better or was still a bad boy, especially now that the skin on his forearm, appear rougher than she remembered. He spent a night with them, left and returned with a bigger bag the next weekend. When Aima questioned him why he came back, he replied that he wanted to spend more time with Dabo before he returned to Nigeria.

"What about work?" Aima asked when they were alone.

"Oh, I am on vacation. In fact, I had already made flight reservations to travel to the United States and spend my vacation there before we met at the hotel."

Aima was relieved. Dabo won't lack company as Odessa would surely give him a tour of France, especially Paris. When they went out, she would take her time at the office to concentrate on her job and her relationship with Pierre without having to bother coming home early to take Dabo out. Recently, she had not seen much of Pierre and that bothered her.

She wondered what might have caused it, "Could it be jealousy? Does he not like Dabo as a family member?" she made a mental note of it and decided she would discuss it with him at the appropriate time.

The next Monday, Aima had a wonderful time at the office. She had been promoted and her colleagues planned to celebrate with her at the company's Club House in the evening. She had to rush home a little early to tell her brother the good news and prepare for the occasion.

On arrival, she found her apartment empty as neither Dabo nor Odessa was home. While taking her bath, she recalled the distortions on Odessa's skin. She kept wondering why it was so rough; with many spots. In fact, the spots looked like scabies.

After her bath, she walked into her bedroom naked from the bathroom. She was not in any particular hurry. She allowed the Night Queen to seep into her skin as she applied it. She creamed her face, neck down to buttocks and legs. Then she sat on her dressing stool in front of a mirror to cream her hands. She was a bit careless with the door; it was ajar. It suddenly occurred to her to lock it for she felt the boys could be back at any moment. Just as she got up from the stool and walked towards the door, a figure ran out from behind it. She grabbed a housecoat from the rack and ran out. Aima saw Odessa and screamed.

Before she could ask him why he was peeping at her naked body from behind the door, he fell on his knees, pleading with her for forgiveness.

"I am really sorry," he cried out. "Please forgive me. I intended knocking but on getting to the door, I noticed it was ajar and saw you creaming your body. I stood transfixed as your beauty struck me like thunderbolt. Please forgive me. It was the devil in me that made me peep into your bedroom."

"Now, stand up!" She commanded.

Dabo heard their voices and rushed into the sitting room where he saw Odessa on his knees.

"Aima, what happened? You came home much earlier today."

Suddenly, she noticed the same infection Odessa had on Dabo's skin. Surprised and exasperated that Dabo had contracted an infectious disease, she stood there speechless and did not even hear his questions.

"Odessa, you go in there, pack your things, leave my house and never come back"

Surprised at the sudden twist, Dabo asked: "What did he do?"

In the place of an answer Aima howled: "Odessa, are you deaf? You leave my house immediately!"

Odessa ran into the room to gather his things. He came out dragging his bag as Dabo tried in vain to mediate.

"Odessa, what happened?" Dabo asked. "Our sister had never been this angry."

Neither Aima nor Odessa offered any explanations to him.

When Odessa left, there was an uneasy silence. Ignorant of the reason behind such an action, Dabo sat on a chair and watched her. He needed to know what had transpired between his sister and their cousin.

"Dabo, what is that mark on your skin?" She asked suddenly.

The question was unexpected and jolted him but he managed to ask: "Where?"

"Can't you see the rashes all over you? I won't take it from you. I simply will not allow it." She emphasized.

Dabo knew the rashes were too obvious for anyone not to notice them. When he discovered them on his skin some days ago, he had wanted to tell her but was not sure how she would take it. His sister was still looking at him angrily, expecting an answer.

"Odessa had been using my bathrobes and towels since he got here. It was just this morning when I woke up that I noticed them." He gazed at her. "Can you imagine I have just four days left to stay in Paris, and I have contracted rashes? How can I go back to Nigeria looking worse than when I left?"

"But I told you I have reservations about Odessa," Aima chided. "Well, now you have no choice. You have to stay here and get that thing treated properly before going back home."

Dabo heaved a sigh of relief. Her reaction surprised him.

"Did you ask Odessa what it is?" She asked with some concern.

"Oh, yes! He said it is scabies and that he contracted it when he went to a bush camp with his friends somewhere in the south of France. They spent three weeks in the camp without taking their bath..."

"What was that for?"

"An annual retreat for a religious sect to which he belongs. Each year he said, they held the retreat in different parts of the world. They believe human beings are free animals. No individual should be unduly influenced by another. A person should have the right to do whatever he or she feels like doing at any point in time as long as it is not criminal. They are free-spirited and always happy.... I know it won't interest you."

"So you thought?" Aima asked angrily. "What if the police were looking for him?" She paused and then continued more gently. "By the way, have I told you the good news? I was promoted today in the office and a party is being organized in my honour this evening. I want you to accompany me. Go and get prepared."

"Congratulations!"

"Thank you."

Dabo rushed into his room as his sister went into hers to dress up. He was the first to finish and waited impatiently for her to come out.

"I am ready!" He called out at last.

"I'm coming," was the response from within.

Dabo went back to his seat and soon, Aima came out looking resplendent.

"Is that all you've got to put on for this occasion?" Aima queried as he stood.

"I like it."

"Okay! We have to wait. Pierre will drive us to the party."

She put on the television and after a while, said: "By the way, I have been thinking about our cousin, Odessa. What benefits does he derive from such a religion?"

"They derive freedom. absolute freedom for believers. People living for today and nothing more. They don't have to worry about tomorrow as no problem is seen as a challenge. Just do whatever you can at any given point in time and leave the rest for Taha…"

"Taha! Who is he?" She questioned.

"Oh, Taha is their goddess. In fact, he said it was the religion that brought him to France from America. It is actually a foreign religion, but when they got to France he loved the place and decided to settle down here. He even told me a ridiculous story of how he lived at the airport for close to one year before he could save enough money to pay for an apartment."

"How is that possible," Aima asked. "Did you believe him?"

"Not that I believe. He said he slept on the arrival lounge couch at night and did cleaning jobs around the airport during the day, using the conveniences of the airport for shelter and bought food off the counter. When you are a Taharist, he said, your spirit is free." He suddenly stopped and reflected: "Don't you see he was practicing Taharism. He could as well live by the riverbank in Abonnema, away from all human habitation."

"Didn't he have other social commitments, no friends?" Aima asked.

"Of course he has. I think if you have any further questions, you have to ask Odessa personally. I have met some of his friends. In fact, I wanted to check out one of his female friends before I realized she was a Taharist. I just made a u-turn and changed the topic."

"Why?"

"Because I believe they have some supernatural powers. Taharist, sense things. I didn't want to start a conversation that could lead to my initiation into the sect."

"When would you have told me this?" Aima asked, shocked.

"Well, I didn't consider it necessary because of the short time I have to stay in France. I figured if I should tell you, you would send Odessa packing. So, I decided to overlook it, thinking he might possibly not pay you a visit in my absence."

"And what makes you think he will not visit?"

"He told me so. He had noticed you don't like him, so he said he would only come around whenever I am present."

Pierre came promptly to pick them for the promotion party. It was fun. Dabo thought they would play only French music and eat only French cuisine. He was wrong. They played makossa, highlife, afro-beat, reggae and some French music. They also served rice the Nigerian way – boiled white rice, served with chicken stew.

The high point of the night was Mr. Pierre's surprise package. He hushed the audience and told them he had an announcement to make. In an atmosphere that screamed with silence, he went down on his knees, brought out an engagement ring and proposed to Aima in the presence of two hundred and fifty eight people. "Will you be my bride?"

Aima was shocked and dumbfounded.

"Say yes! Say yes!" Everyone screamed.

Aima's heart refused. When she looked at Pierre and those pleading eyes, she didn't want to disgrace him in the presence of that crowd. She looked up and instead of saying yes, started a long thank you speech. Pierre

was still on his knees. At the end of the speech, she looked at him, and in an atmosphere one could cut with a knife, bent down and whispered to him: "We shall discuss it later."
Pierre got the message and reluctantly got to his feet and Aima, with a mischievous glint in her eyes looked straight at him and announced gaily.
"Yes, I will."

There was a long round of applause in the hall.

CHAPTER 11

The atmosphere in the car was tensed as Pierre drove Aima and her brother back home. Their thoughts were running amok. Aima was confused. She never expected what happened at the party. She was aware of all the resentment of his family and the struggle to keep their relationship going. "Why must he force a marriage on me in a party of all places? There are many issues yet to be settled," she mused.

Pierre kept replaying the near-embarrassment in his mind. "Why was Aima hesitant," he kept wondering. "What is it that she would want to discuss with me? And why later?" He recalled all the quarrels he had had with his family because of her. His mother couldn't come to terms with the fact that he was in love with a coloured woman. On many occasions, she had asked him: "What has happened to all our girls?" Pierre had been in difficulty giving her a satisfactory answer. She had looked forward to having a daughter-in-law she could proudly take to her fancy tea parties. His own sister had told him he had gone mad.

At the traffic light, they stopped. The light was still showing red when he drove off, almost hitting another car.

"Zut! Zut!" He exclaimed.

"Mais fais attention!" Aima cried out.

They got to Aima's house in time and without any other incident. She made to jump out of the car as soon as it came to a halt, but Pierre stopped her. He stretched out his right hand and placed it on her left, expecting her to understand she had to wait for Dabo to get down from the car first.

"What was wrong?" Pierre asked her as Dabo alighted from the car.

"What exactly are you talking about?" She questioned, feigning ignorance.

"Your long speech and reluctance to accept my proposal." Retorted Pierre.

"But I accepted, didn't I?" She asked with a smile.

She waited, rubbing the back of her right hand on her nose. Pierre recounted how he almost made water in his pants because he thought she was going to say 'no' to his proposal.

"Don't you love me, Aima?" He asked finally with a tremulous voice.

"Pierre, listen to me. I love you… I really do. In Africa, marriage goes beyond a decision between a man and a woman; it involves two families. You have proposed. I advise you to deliberate with your own family while I do same with mine. If our families permit, I will marry you."

"Are you suggesting you would travel down to Nigeria to discuss my proposal first with your family before making up your mind? That's no love, Aima. If you love me, you should not hesitate in saying 'yes.' I'd just call my family and announce the good news. Anyway, I will give you sometime to make up your mind."

As Aima smiled, Pierre became upset and admonished: "I hope you are not making a mockery of my love for you."

Aima caressed his face.

"Pierre, listen, I am tired. Why can't we continue this discussion some other time…"

"When?" He interrupted. "I'm sorry if I have stressed you, but I need to know if you are interested in me or not."

"I promise." She kissed him. "Bonne nuit." She said in a hushed voice.

"Bonne nuit." He responded.

"Call me tomorrow," she repeated as she alighted from the car.

Aima was almost at her door when Pierre responded: "I will."

Two weeks later, Dabo left for Nigeria.

****

At Petromina's release, the inner caucus of TBK Nigeria Limited celebrated their victory. They had committed all sorts of crime; from drug trafficking to prostitution and had never been caught. There was nothing to link them to any of such errant behaviour. Members of their staff were well trained and they carried out many investigations and underground work before they took up any client.

Her case almost blew their cover. In the end, Terrence was pleased with Fredrick. They were all glad it was over. Fredrick knew they should forget everything about Petromina and put the whole incidence behind them but he could not. At first he thought Petromina was nothing but a disappointment because of her blunder; He had certainly overestimated her intelligence. Later this feeling changed to respect and gratitude for she had not tried to implicate him or any other person for that matter. Then he realized he had fallen in love with her. She was always on his mind. How was he going to achieve the feat of getting her to be his girl? He made some enquiries and learnt that she had gone back to her parents. That posed a bit of a challenge because he knew a man could not just knock on a girl's door in her parents' house. This is Africa. He decided to enlist the help of his sister, Miracle, who was about the same age as Petromina.

****

Miss Miracle Sunday lodged in Crown Hotel, not too far from Petromina's house in the village. She spent two days watching Petromina's movement from her hotel room. On the third day, she got out of the hotel earlier than Petromina and walked in the direction of her quarry's house. From her calculations, Petromina should have come out of her house about that time, but unfortunately for her, she hadn't. Miss Sunday stood outside, some distance away from the house for a while then went back to her hotel room.

She repeated this process every other day until she spotted Petromina on her fifth attempt. Miracle walked straight to her and pretending she needed directions, accosted her. Petromina gave her the directions and left. Two days later they stumbled on each other again.

"Hi, my name is Miracle. Friends call me Mira."

"I am Petromina or simply Pet." She said with a smile and kept walking as if she was in a hurry.

"You gave me directions some days back, have you forgotten?" Miracle asked.

"Oh! Don't mind me," said Petromina. "I am not too good at remembering faces. Sorry about that. Hope to see you some other time, and what did you say your name was?"

"Miracle."

"Petromina," she replied and hurried off.

Miracle tailed Petromina and saw her opening a make-shift store at the entrance of Abagana market. She watched quietly as she brought out a coal pot made of a white-washed basin with charcoal in it. She went back in and brought out three stools, dropped them on the ground, looked up, and greeted a passer-by. Then she placed the basin on one of the stools and sat on a second, as if expecting someone.

About twenty minutes later, an elderly woman came by carrying a bunch of ripe and unripe plantains on her head and a big sack in her right hand.

"Welcome mama." Petromina greeted.

"Why have you not started the fire yet?" Asked her mum.

"Mama, today is very windy. It seems as if it's going to rain."

"Okay, let's watch it a bit," she considered.

Petromina helped her mum with the things she had brought back from the market. The sack contained a pot of tomatoes gravy, fresh fish, ground fresh pepper, a jerry can of palm oil and some salt. Petromina swept the area, made the fire in the coal pot, placed and covered it with wire gauze and then placed the pot of gravy on a corner of the gauze.

Her mother brought out fresh fish, cut them to size, cleaned and marinated them with fresh pepper, palm oil and salt. She then placed the pieces of fish on the gauze to roast. Together they washed and peeled the entire plantain one after the other, and also placed them on the gauze.

At this point, Miracle went back to her hotel room to call Mr. Fredrick Sunday.

"Hello, is that TBK Nigeria Limited?"

"Yes, may I help you?" Asked the receptionist.

"Can I speak to Mr. Fredrick Sunday please?"

"Who should I say wants to speak with him?"

"Tell him Miracle Sunday, his sister."

"Okay, wait a moment."

Not long, Fredrick came on the line.

"Yes, Fredrick on the line… how far, Mira?"

"I know where she lives and works," she said.

"She works already?" Asked a surprised Fredrick.

'Not really."

"What do you mean, Mira? Stop beating about the bush."

"Her mum sells roast plantain and fish in the market and Petromina helps her out." She explained.

"That is good. Proceed to the second level of the plan," instructed Fredrick.

"Brother, I need some money. I didn't know I will stay this long."

"Okay! I will send some money to you. Obi, my colleague, will bring it to you tomorrow."

The next day, Miracle again went to the market. This time she went straight to Petromina and asked for the price of the roast plantain.

"You are here again?" Observed Petromina.

"Yes. This time you have recognized me." She continued "Why is such a beautiful girl like you doing this?"

"I am just helping out my mother."

"Where is she?" Asked Miracle.

"She went inside the market to buy some more plantain for roasting."

"I want to buy two roast plantain and fish. I will sit here and eat."

Petromina brought out two of the plantain on the hot gauze and cleaned them with a knife. She brought out a metal plate and then used her bare fingers to break the plantain into smaller bits. Thereafter, she added gravy with two pieces of roast fish. Miracle paid, sat by her and ate.

"Are you new in the village?" Asked Petromina.

Miracle hesitated before answering: "Yes, I am new. I'm staying in the hotel."

At the mention of a hotel, Petromina's interest grew. She looked at her and asked: "Why do you stay in a hotel?"

"Because I live in Port Harcourt," explained the other. "I only come here on a visit and since I don't know anybody here, I lodge in the hotel whenever I am here."

Miracle had expected Petromina to inform her she also lived in Port Harcourt but that was not forthcoming. Rather, she thanked her for her patronage and company. She felt disappointed. Petromina is in dire need of company as her sojourn in Port Harcourt hadn't removed the stigma of an outcast and the isolation and degradation that goes with it.

"I will visit you in the hotel." She announced suddenly.

This statement revived Miracle's hopes. This could be an opportunity and she would not fail to exploit it.

"Oh! You will be very welcome. You know, I feel so lonely in the hotel."

"At this point, Petromina's mother returned so Miracle washed her hands and left. For three days Petromina did not show up at the hotel and Miracle, finally exasperated, returned to Port Harcourt.

CHAPTER 12

Dabo arrived in Port Harcourt from France with sweet memories. He has exciting stories to tell and told his people that in France, people went about half-dressed. That what the girls generally wore was not bigger than wash-clothes, while in the summer, they wore skimpy clothes. To his siblings, he lamented that although Aima dressed decently to work, she was no different from the rest. He informed them that they would not recognize her if they saw her because she was as thin as a broomstick.

"I am not sure my sister can live in Nigeria again. She has so much changed. She speaks French like the French people and all her friends are white. If not for the colour of her skin, one would think she is from that country. She drives a posh car and hardly eats. She also wears her hair long and flowing."

Their mother was sad. The sudden distortion on her face bore evidence to her sorrow.

"That's the price one pays for success. If I had known, I would have dissuaded Aima from moving to France. I know she loves beautiful things but I never knew Aima could be influenced to the point of almost becoming a white lady. It means she will eventually marry a Frenchman and we would never see her again. Dabo, does she have any man in her life?"

"Yes. He is a Frenchman, named Pierre. The relationship is not going well. There is always tension between them. When I was there, I observed that Aima was always edgy when he was around. I am not sure my sister is truly in love with him."

"Observer," Moty interrupted. "When are you getting married yourself?"

"As soon as I date the right girl," Dabo responded.

"And when are you going to start searching," snapped their mother.

"I have seen her, but I have not approached her yet."

"That's interesting. Do I know her?" His mother asked.

"Maybe," he replied. "But it is my little secret. You will know at the appropriate time."

"When will that be?" She insisted.

"She slipped out of my fingers; when I find her again, you will be the first to know."

"Joker! I should never have taken you seriously."

Having said this, Ibiye left the room.

******

Miracle had never been known for her patience and Petromina was beginning to annoy her. She did not know what her brother saw in this village girl that had gotten herself involved in a drug case. Even though she won the case, Miracle believed there was 'no smoke without fire.' Why should any drug baron pick Petromina out of a million girls? And why should it be the same girl her brother wanted to marry at all cost? She had always known her brother was weird but she never knew he was also insane. Any normal man would want to keep a distance from such a girl. The most annoying part for Miracle was, having to make friends with Petromina, a village girl who had no class. After she refused to pay her a visit, Miracle left for Port Harcourt in anger.

In Port Harcourt, she went straight to her house, dropped her luggage, and headed for her brother's office. At the customers' services, she asked the Customer Relations Officer, Mary John, if she could see Fredrick.

"And you are?" Mary asked.

"I am Miracle. I want to see Fredrick."

"You can wait for about twenty minutes, he is in a meeting."

"That's okay by me," Miracle responded.

When she eventually saw Fredrick, Miracle asked him when the company intends to get rid of the customers' relations officer.

"Any time from now baby," he replied.

"You said so four months ago."

"We have not seen a suitable person yet. I might as well offer the post to Petromina. What do you think?"

Miracle flinched. "Everybody who comes here complains about Mary. Each time I come here she would say: 'You are looking for Fredrick.' She never says: 'Are you looking for Fredrick?'"

They both laughed.

"Now tell me about Petromina. Did you see her?" Fredrick asked suddenly.

Miracle told him Petromina stood her up. She said she was tired of playing goody with her and was no longer going to assist him; she was quitting.

"What is so special about that girl?" She asked. "She is not even half as pretty as your other girls. I find her a snub."

Fredrick explained he felt that following the police incident, Petromina would take her time to warm up to people. He imagined she would either be suspicious of every stranger that crossed her path or she would simply shy away from them. He pleaded with her to try again.

"This time a different approach is needed," he pleaded.

"And what would be my gain in all this?" She queried.

"I will express my gratitude financially if you succeed."

*   *   *   *

Money, they say, is a catalyst and two days later, Miracle was back to the market where Petromina sold roast plantain. She was fortunate to find her again but this time, took her time considering the best form of approach.

"Hi, Pet!" She greeted, smiling broadly.

"Hi, Mira, do you want to buy plantain?"

"No, I came to see you. Why didn't you visit as you promised?"

"Sorry, I forgot. I have many irons in the fire. Apart from assisting my mama here, I also do job-hunting and attend interviews. At the end of the day, I get very tired."

"Have you any offers yet?"

"No...not yet."

"Why?"

"I guess I didn't do well in any of the interviews."

"If you are offered a job in Port Harcourt, will you take it?"

"No. I had a terrible experience there. I don't think anyone would agree to give me employment. I bet that is what is affecting my chances here."

Miracle saw a window of opportunity in this statement and was determined to exploit it. It was a resolution, informed by the promise of financial rewards.

"Well, Miracle said, my brother works for this company; they need a new customers' relations officer and I think you are suitable for the job. I will put in a word for you."

"Do you know what chased me away from Port Harcourt?"

"No!" Miracle replied. "What offence did you commit? You didn't steal or kill, did you?"

"No. I am not a criminal," she replied "I was innocently roped into what would have been a crime."

Petromina then narrated all her experience in Port Harcourt.

"You live in Port Harcourt, why didn't you know about it?" She asked.

"Well, I heard about it but didn't know the name or names of the people involved. Besides, I don't read the papers. Well, I don't think you will have any problem, after all, you were vindicated in the end."

"Why are you so nice to me?"

"I am just being myself," Miracle replied. "In fact, I went back to Port Harcourt last week. When my brother told me about the vacancy in his office, I remembered you and came back to inform you."

"Why didn't you apply for the job yourself?"

"I didn't apply for some reasons. Firstly, I am at the university and secondly, the company policy does not permit two members of the same family to be employed; and thirdly, I am not cut out for the office environment. I can go on and on… any way, think about the offer. I am leaving for Port Harcourt tomorrow, come and see me if you are interested."

This, of course, was a bluff. Had Petromina not showed up, Miracle would have devised another means to convince her.

Miracle went back to Port Harcourt in the company of Petromina. Having agreed to meet at TBK Nigeria Limited the next morning, they retired to their different homes.

Petromina was fortunate the rent on her house had not expired. After all the scandal, she initially never intended returning to Port Harcourt. She thought she could look for work somewhere else and then return to pack her things. Unfortunately, that was not possible. Even though she was vindicated and cleared of the charges, many people still did not believe she was totally innocent.

Her residence in Amos Street in Mile 2 Diobu, now wore a different look. "Where are all the children that usually cluster around the street to play?" She wondered. Even mama Jane, the akara (bean cake) seller, was not under the mango tree. The mallams (petty traders from Northern Nigeria), who sold cigarettes and beverages were also gone. As she approached her house, No. 20, the picture seemed to get clearer. She also noticed the street had been graded and tarred. Where the children used to play and mallam's kiosk used to be, had been replaced by a few cars and motorcycles parked there by new tenants.

She finally got home. At first, she was scared. The premises now had a fence and a gate. She noticed many mallams or abokis, clustering at the gatehouse as if they were in a meeting.

Eunice saw her before the other neighbourhood kids.

"Aunty Pet is back! Aunty Pet is back!" Shouted the kids as they all ran towards her.

One of them held her bag while another held her hand.

"Welcome aunty!" They chorused.

"How are you children? You have all grown so tall. What have you all been eating?"

"Garri and soup," Eunice answered.

"Lucy, why are you so fat?" Asked Petromina.

"She has been eating too much beans," joked one of the boys.

"Aunty, we have not had a drink of Coke or Fanta since you disappeared," commented Gina.

"Who told you she disappeared, didn't you know she was in trouble?" Eunice questioned.

"Who told you I was in trouble?" Petromina asked anxiously.

"Everybody said it. Many people believed you were innocent, but some said they don't know."

"How old are you, Eunice?"

"Thirteen years in two weeks time."

"Now that I am back, we will celebrate."

They went with her towards her room but couldn't get in because an additional lock had been added. Ken, the landlord's son offered an explanation.

"Papa told them to put an additional lock on your door when they were renovating the house. He said with that you would not sneak in and out of your room and later hold him responsible for any loss of your property."

Petromina was deeply embarrassed but didn't respond. "That's the price one pays for getting involved in crime, she mused."

Ken went to their flat and brought the spare key for Petromina who opened the door and they all went in excitedly. She brought out snacks she had bought for the kids on her way and shared it among them.

Almost immediately, word went round that Petromina is back. Her female neighbours started arriving one after the other. Everybody welcomed her at the same time. They asked if she had come to stay for good, to which she answered in the affirmative. The landlord's wife brought a meal of boiled yam and stew for her because she knew Petromina would be hungry from her journey. She thanked her and ate amidst talks, questions, answers and much laughter.

Petromina kept recounting the story of what happened and how God had saved her. People came and went. Some came with good intentions, while others came to take away information for gossip. One of the women even remarked that Petromina was looking uglier and emaciated: "She must have passed through hell," she concluded.

CHAPTER 13

The following morning, as she walked towards the gates of TBK Nigeria Limited, Petromina felt intimidated. Before she got here, she was happy and almost certain she had got a job because of Mira's promise. But when she saw the marbled office, she became unsure. "How could Mira be so confident that her services would be needed here? Unless, of course, the company belongs to her father or husband," she thought.

She told herself it was too early to be pessimistic and she walked through the gates, in between the row of parked cars. Just as she was getting confused about the location of the entrance, a glass door opened automatically and a unformed security guard, smartly dressed in a white shirt that had two red strips of rank on the shoulder with a navy-blue trousers having red stripes at the sides and complemented with a navy-blue cap, ushered her in.

Once in the building, Petromina did not need further directions. Every table was tagged. The waiting area had three tables; one for the security guard, the second for the customers' relations officer, while the third table was for the messenger.

The visitors' seats consist of three separate three-sitter leather sofas. The hall had a magazine rack and a colour television set. The television set alternated between CNN and a tour of TBK Nigeria Limited. She walked straight to the customers' relations officer.

"Please, I have an appointment to meet Miracle here. She is not a member of your staff but said I should wait for her here when I arrive."

"You are?" The lady asked.

"I am Petromina Okoye."

"You came to see Miracle?"

"Yes," answered Petromina. "Do you know her?"

"The visit is official?"

"Yes, but I have to see Mira first."

"You can wait for her?"

"Yes, I can."

"Then, sit here," she said, pointing to one of the sofas.

Petromina wondered why such a beautiful office could have such a boring and unprofessional receptionist. She fervently prayed to be employed. From the look of the decorations, she knew her salary would be good. Just then, Miracle walked in, apologizing for her lateness.

"Have you dropped your application?" She asked.

"No, I was waiting for you."

"You shouldn't have waited. Let me have it."

Petromina brought it out from her hand bag and gave it to her friend who handed it over to the receptionist. They waited for a while before the receptionist called Petromina into an interview room while Mira waited at the reception.

Within an hour, the interview had been concluded and she was surprisingly given employment with a letter to confirm it. She was asked to resume duty the following day. Her job had nothing to do with the shady deals in the company. She underwent training and replaced the boring CRO.

******

Fredrick was away on an assignment outside Port Harcourt. On his return, he was happy to learn that Petromina had started work. Miracle went back to school. Petromina promised to visit her as soon as she received her first salary. She also planned to look for Dabo and render her apologies to him. He was just at the wrong place at the wrong time.

As was customary with the company, the staff was informed by a memo when there was a new member and the date such a person would be introduced to other members of staff. Petromina was introduced on Friday, during the staff meeting.

Fredrick rushed through his engagements to make himself available for the staff meeting. His office was in a different section from Petromina's and so she did not see him in the morning when she resumed.

During the staff meeting, she was rudely shocked and almost passed out when she saw him. Only Fredrick noticed the look on her face. She wondered what Fredrick was looking for in such a corporate environment. She was sure nobody knew he had a dubious character. She knew he had got her into the suspected mess. She became fidgety and uncomfortable but by the time the meeting ended, her nerves had calmed though her heart was still racing like a train. Just as she was wondering if there were no safe hideouts in the world, Fredrick walked up to her.

"Hi, Pet, don't be scared, I am a friend not an enemy. I will talk to you later."

"How did he know my name?" She wondered. "Oh! How stupid of me! I had just been introduced to the whole staff," but she could not remember shortening her name. She had told them her full names; Petromina Okoye. Only her friends or people she considered as close, called her Pet.

She got home still jittery and tired. She was too worried and tired to even change her clothes. She went straight to her bed and fell into a deep sleep. That night, she dreamt. In her dream she attended a Christian wedding in a four star hotel. Both the service and the reception were held in the hotel. This was a rarity in this part of the world. People have an old-fashioned belief that God dwells only in churches, so to hold a service in a hotel was strange. Strangely, she did not know the bride or the groom. She had been invited by Dabo who happened to be her friend in the dream. He told her the bride was his kid sister who lived abroad. She even recognized a couple of people she knew in Port Harcourt.

There were also many dignitaries. Petromina accompanied Miracle in her car to the wedding. At the wedding reception, many souvenirs were given out. People ignored her and gave souvenirs to only people they knew.

She felt very lonely. Even Miracle whom she had accompanied to the wedding seemed to have disappeared. Meanwhile, her handbag and gift for the couple were in Miracle's car.

Petromina decided to walk up to Dabo. After all, he had invited her. Unfortunately though, he seemed to be very busy and there were always many people around him. Later, she decided to look out for Mira and head home.

Just as she came out of the wedding hall, she saw Dabo with many people around him. They were congratulating him on the wedding of his younger sister and at the same time, sympathizing with him on the death of his elder sister. Tears ran down his cheeks. She stood glued to the spot, and just then he saw her. Dabo apologized for not paying much attention to her throughout the duration of the ceremony. He asked what she was looking for and she told him her friend, who had given her a lift to the wedding had abandoned her and left. He asked one of his aunts to be on standby to take Petromina home in her car in case the latter did not find Miracle.

Petromina woke up from her sleep the following morning, feeling much better. Finding Dabo was top on her agenda. When she had swept her room, she went outside with a bucket to fetch water from the only tap that existed in the entire premises. She promised herself she would move out of this apartment when her three year tenancy period expires – she still had about six months to go. She had decided that her next apartment would have the necessary comforts like running water, water heater in both the bathroom and kitchen and a lot of other things.

She fetched the water, went inside and had a cold bath. Thereafter, she got dressed and fixed a breakfast of plantain, scrambled eggs and a cup of tea. She needed to regain her energy for the dream had exhausted her. Until now, she had believed people dreamt in black-and-white, but she vividly remembered the lovely red dress Mira had worn in the dream. Even the bride's friends had worn exotic peach-coloured dresses. The whole dream was bitter-sweet!

****

Aima called from France. She was excited and happy, having graduated in flying colours. Aima had been pursuing a part-time doctorate degree programme. Now she was Dr. Aima

Richardson. She announced that she would come home briefly to spend time with them, news that made the whole family very happy.

Ibiye, her mum, thanked God and blessed the heavens. Because it was a Saturday, everybody was present at home and they all took turns to speak with Aima. Everybody made one demand or the other. Dr. Richardson asked her to buy him a bowler hat and sossorobi perfume. Her siblings asked her to buy them the clothes and shoes in vogue. Dabo warned Angel to specify what sort of attire she needed since he was certain that should Aima apply her discretion in the choice of clothes, Angel would not be able to wear what Aima would buy.

"Why?" Angel questioned.

"Because what Aima would buy will be too skimpy for you to wear in this society."

"I don't care, Dabo. I want to look and dress like Aima. Everybody will want to meet Aima when she gets back and I will like to wear the sort of things she wears so they won't think I am a bush girl."

"Okay Angel, please yourself," Dabo continued. "Don't say I did not warn you."

****

Petromina went to the club earlier than the habitual clubbers. She met with her former colleagues, chatted and exchanged hugs. She noticed the club had employed many new hands. Even the manager of the club embraced her. Meanwhile, he was hoping she had not come back to seek reemployment. When they started chatting, he learnt she was back in Port Harcourt and had only stopped by to see them and catch some fun. Each of her former colleagues had a question or two to ask her as they went about their daily routine. Joe, the bar attendant got the bulk of the gist because she sat at the bar area.

She had decided not to ask any of them about Dabo. Rather, she would sit till late hoping he would stop by. She reasoned that if he did not appear she would repeat her visit on Friday night. From past experience, she knew Fridays were his favourite club nights. If he still failed to show, she would look for him in his place of work. Luckily for her, she did not have to wait long before he appeared.

Dabo took his siblings out that night to celebrate Aima's success. One of the places they went to was Ashama Night Club. As he walked in with his siblings, he saw her seated on a stool at the bar.

"That would not be Pet," he thought. Since his release, he had visited the nightclub a couple of times. On few occasions, he'd asked after her but nobody had any information of her. They said they had not seen her since the scandal and that they were not sure if she would ever come back to the club. The manager even said he will not employ her again even if she came back because he was not sure of how his customers would react to her presence. Her case had been all over the news. Meanwhile, only a few of the papers had carried the good news of her release.

Petromina sat quietly on the stool, sipping her lemonade at intervals. She watched Dabo walk into the club with two people for company. She wasn't sure he had seen her. If he did, he did not show any indication. She knew he would go to his favourite table; he did. She decided to allow him settle down and approach him at an appropriate moment. She also never gave any indication of seeing him come in.

Her seat was at a vantage position. For a difference, she was a customer not a staffer. Then just as she was about to go to Dabo, she saw another regular group at the opposite end of the room. They too were at their usual table. For the first time, the whole puzzle started falling into place. She saw Fredrick seated at his favourite table with some friends. No wonder he looked familiar at the shopping mall. He always wore a hat that covered his forehead whenever he was at the nightclub. She had never taken special notice of him. She seldom waited on customers at that end of the club. They were always loud and noisy, always staying in groups and spent money as if it grew on trees. No wonder he had picked on her.

Seeing him brought back memories. She recalled a particular day when Azuka, the regular staffer that covered that section of the hall, had fallen ill and she had to attend to customers in that section in addition to her regular duties. She remembered receiving a tip of three thousand naira that night. That was the highest she had ever received and had thanked him profusely. He had asked her why she was thanking him that much and she had replied that it was not everyday somebody gave her half of a month's salary, as tip. They asked her if she would accept a better paying job if she was offered one, and she had laughed and asked: "Who dash monkey banana?" She implied that it was almost unimaginable to have a better paying job with her limited education. She never took special notice of him because the section he sat was dimly lit. After that conversation, she was only privileged to serve in that corner, once in a long while.

Petromina was still reminiscing when she was startled by a voice close to her ears.

"Hello stranger, can I buy you a drink?"

"Hi, Dabo, long time no see," she replied.

"I noticed you are lonely and decided to come and keep you company. Where did you steal my heart to all these months?"

Petromina could not believe her ears. When she left her house in search of him, her intention was to render apologies. She did not know how she would go about it, but she never figured it would be this easy.

"I went straight to my village after I was released. I needed to relocate but unfortunately, nobody wanted to employ an ex-convict till a friend of mine got me a place in TBK Nigeria Limited."

"Male or female friend?" He asked, curious.

"What does it matter to you?"

"It matters because you have the other half of my heart." He continued, "It is good to see you on this side of the counter. Come and sit with us and thank you for testifying truthfully."

"I actually came to look out for you here. I am sorry for all the mess I got you into," she confessed.

"Apology accepted. Come and meet my siblings."

She obliged him.

"Hi, I am Petromina."

"I am Angel and this is my brother Emmanuel."

Petromina did not miss the exchange of glances between them. One would think Petromina was bad news. She was grateful they kept whatever opinion they had of her to themselves and remained polite all through the night. Dabo and Petromina exchanged addresses before they left for their different destinations.

CHAPTER 14

The following Monday, Fredrick invited Petromina to lunch. She was hesitant but he assured her it was going to be strictly official and she finally obliged him. They went to an eatery known for its local delicacies situated only two streets from the office and had a good meal of pounded yam and fresh fish in palm oil soup. This is a Port Harcourt delicacy. After the meal, they talked.

Fredrick apologized for the troubles he had caused her. He told her the powder stuff was actually meant to be a joke. He was not a drug dealer, but wanted to test her IQ for a very sensitive job and the best way to test her was to do it secretly. He reminded her of the night they had talked about her willingness to do a better paying job. She now asked him what the new job entailed, but he told her that since she had failed the test, there was no need telling her about a job she would have had. Besides, he wanted all discussions about that night to end that day. He had compensated her with this her new job.

"Compensate me?" She questioned.

"Yes. I sent Miracle to search you out."

"Mira sounded genuine and sweet although I always sensed she was holding back something. So everything was a lie?"

"No! Mira doesn't know beyond getting you back to Port Harcourt to pick up this new job."

"Why are you doing this? What is the catch?"

"Just paying for the mess I got you into. You sealed your lips and I am very proud of you."

"Is that all?" She asked.

"I developed a fondness for you over the months but I see I am already too late. I shouldn't have wasted time playing the good boy."

"What do you mean?"

"I saw you at the club on Saturday night with that guy... what's his name again?"

"Dabo," she reminded him.

"Yes, Dabo."

"There is nothing between us."

Her instincts told her Fredrick was not telling her everything. She remembered the gun he carried on the night he smuggled the powder into her bag and also recalled her dream. She decided she would tread carefully. He got her once; he was not going to get her again.

"Why did you bring me to this buka to eat, instead of the office cafeteria?"

"This is what we call medicine after death."

"Why?"

"Because you are asking me after you have devoured the meal," he chuckled and continued: "People gossip much. You see, no one knew I brought you into the company. If they do, they would not be comfortable to talk in your presence. They would think you are my girl." He explained.

"But is that not what you want?"

"To be my girlfriend or the gossip?"

She ignored his question and picked her teeth, while Fredrick watched her, willing her to accept.

"So will you be my girl?" He pressured.

She opened her mouth to speak but shut it with a sigh. She picked another tooth but was wise enough to conceal her mouth with her left palm. Afterwards, she looked at him and said: "Not for now. Give me time to gather myself. Everything is happening too fast"

******

Dabo also invited Petromina out the following weekend. They went to Ndoki Beach. It was a beautiful place; an exotic blend of man-made African architecture and nature. The beach was not for swimming although one could fish in it. It had fifteen detached chalets by the waterfront. Each chalet had a burnt-brick barbeque stand with charcoal in them placed at strategic corners outside. Dabo had paid for a chalet for the day.

They got there in the morning, had a long chat, ate breakfast at the central eating spot and went back to the chalet to watch the Oprah Winfrey show on cable television. Thereafter, they slept.

They were woken up by the sound of loud drumbeats. From their balcony, they had a good view of the traditional dance display on parade that day. The climax of the dance was the owigiri. Everyone was invited to join in this. They all danced till late in the night.

For dinner, they bought barbequed fish and plantain and sat on the sand at the waterfront, fully clothed to eat and chat. They seemed to talk about every topic under the sun. By midnight, she asked him to take her home. He protested, saying he had paid for a whole day and it would be wrong to waste that much money. She asked why he did not take her to his own home and he lied he still lived with his parents. It would be disrespectful to spend the night with her under their roof, he concluded.

In truth, everybody in the house disliked her. They thought she was bad news. His younger ones had told their parents about their encounter with her. Dabo told his parents they were just casual friends and they advised him not allow their relationship to go beyond the platonic.

****

Dabo picked Aima up from the Port Harcourt International Airport exactly two weeks after her call. Her flight arrived at about 7 am. He went with Petromina so that she could keep him company while he waited for the flight. He however believed the flight might not arrive at the scheduled time, because flights into Nigeria were hardly punctual. But this particular flight proved him wrong.

They heard the flight arrival announcement as soon as they got to the airport. Petromina was shocked when she saw Aima; she was the girl she had seen in her dream and she wore the same lovely red dress. She could not understand the mystery. This was no ordinary dream, yet she could not interpret it. The second surprise was the number of suitcases Aima had. She silently counted them; thirteen. "Why on earth would somebody carry all these suitcases?" She wondered.

Dabo made the introductions and the two ladies shook hands and exchanged pleasantries. Aima had not known Petromina was the girl that got Dabo into trouble and was very sweet and polite to her. They went into Dabo's Toyota Tarcel car and drove off.

On the way home, Aima kept sneezing and complaining.

"Oh, this place stinks. Oh, this! Oh, that!" She complained. "The sun is burning too hot, why? See how the roads are littered... see that poor little girl hawking bread. Dabo, don't you see that poor little girl hawking bread? Do you think that girl is up to six years old?"

"Aima! Welcome back home," interjected Dabo.

"Yeah, home, sweet home," she commented.

"Stop complaining. Nothing has changed much since you left."

"Ah, bon!"

Everybody was waiting at home when they arrived. Dabo had dropped Petromina off on the way so it would be strictly a family affair.

Ibiye got the first hug from Aima, followed by the others.

"My queen, see how thin you are. Don't you people eat in France?" Ibiye asked.

"They are very health conscious there." Her daughter answered.

"But you are too thin."

"Mum, this is every girl's dream figure over there."

"I would have passed you on the way without recognizing my own daughter."

"Ah, bon!"

"Your hair is as long as that of a white lady, and almost as grey as your grandfather's except the colour is slightly different."

Angel, who had been watching the drama between mother and daughter, interjected.

"And she has cat eyes. So this whole package is what you call fashion; long blonde hair, size eight dress and blue contact lenses?"

"Beauty, fashion, this, that. France has certainly impacted on you. I hope you don't smoke like them?" Ibiye contributed.

"Bon!

"You look gorgeous, my queen." complimented her father. "Come and give me another hug."

She ran into his arms and afterwards, embraced her siblings again.

Ibiye had prepared a sumptuous meal of yam, boiled in dry fish peppered soup, and served in palm oil. They all had to wait for Aima to freshen up before they could begin their meal. The whole family chatted happily as they tried to catch up on things over the meal. After the meal, they suggested Aima take a short nap after which, she could conclude her tale.

After two hours, she came out of her bedroom wearing a pair of tightly fitted trousers and a skimpy top with spaghetti straps.

"Why are you coming out of your room in your underwear?" Her mum asked.

"Underwear? No, this is not underwear it is summer wear. I never noticed how hot this country was before I left for Europe."

"Neither were you aware of how it stank or how merchandise is hawked in the streets, and so many other things," Dabo added mischievously.

Don't be sarcastic, Dabo. Aima just got back and she is bound to notice many things," chided Angel.

"If the observation is negative, she should keep it to herself, especially when she cannot change the situation." Dabo insisted. "When I arrived in France, the whole airport seemed perfumed. I didn't make a fuss about it; neither did I complain of the cold that made me feel as if air conditioners were installed in every street in the city." He paused and then added. "What is more, they have attitudinal problems over there. Daddy, could you believe that a young woman fell at the arrival lounge of the airport and people were sniggering instead of helping her?"

"In France, especially Paris, everybody minds his or her business," Aima cut in, defending her country of residence. "Besides, no one wants to be seen as a busybody; involving themselves in something that doesn't concern them. That would be impertinent."

"Since when does helping someone in need become disrespectful? I advise, you mind your choice of words. But getting down to brass tacks, I think every country and her people have their own challenges, so stop complaining.

"Ah, bon!

Don't worry, Aima. You will feel much better when Power Holding Company of Nigeria (P.H.C.N.), brings back the power, then you can switch on the air conditioner. We know in France, there is no power failure as long as one paid his bills." Emmanuel interjected sarcastically.

"Don't worry pop," Aima said, looking at her dad. "I will get you a power generating set before I go back. That way, you won't feel the heat or dark when P.H.C.N. strikes."

"Thank you sweet heart, but we are now used to it," her father said.

Aima gave everyone what she'd brought for them and the family stayed indoors throughout the day to further catch up on lost times.

Many visitors came to welcome Aima, and to congratulate her on her achievements. They all went back with gifts, old Mrs. Boro numbered among them. She no longer looked sophisticated as Aima had considered her to be. "Maybe I am comparing her to my European colleagues," she conceded.

On Sunday, they held a thanks giving service in Aima's honour, to celebrate her various achievements and acknowledge God's mercies on the Richardsons'. The occasion was a huge success.

Later, when the children were alone, they discussed their relationships with the opposite sex. Aima confessed she was confused about her feelings for Pierre and was not ready to make any commitment yet. Dabo divulged he was in love with Petromina, but did not know how to tell his parents about it. Angel told him it would be a daunting task, getting their parents permission to marry her. She'd heard them discussing Petromina. Their mum had complained she was an osu – an outcast – and worse still, a call girl in a night club. She had emphasized that Dabo was of royal descent and definitely would not allow him stoop so low as to marry Petromina.

"We are not Igbos." Dabo had said on that occasion. "Osu or no osu has nothing to do with us; The Kalabari culture doesn't forbid us from marrying an osu. We don't even know what the osu caste system is about.

"If not for nosy Mrs. Boro, mum wouldn't have over-reacted like this." Belema, his sister, chipped in.

"But was she a call girl?" Aima asked.

"No, but she worked at a nightclub." Moty answered.

"Aima, did you know she was the same girl that got him in trouble with the police?" Emmanuel asked.

"I didn't know that. But love, they say, is blind. Brother, if you love her, then by all means, go for her. You have my blessings." Aima encouraged.

"Who are you and what blessings are you talking about?" Angel queried.

"Are you not an African? Have you ever seen where a man and a woman just went ahead with a marriage ceremony without the consent of their parents and family members?"

Just then they heard their mother's footsteps and changed the topic since it was considered improper to discuss intimate relationships before elders.

In fact, in Kalabari tradition as in most African cultures, couples are not even supposed to court. If a man sees any lady he admires and wishes to marry, the proper thing is to inform his parents. They in turn, will send people to investigate the family of the girl; up to her lineage.

The purpose of the investigation is to know who exactly the girl is in terms of attitude and character. It was also meant to find out if she has a good family background; especially who her parents and forebears are. For instance, do they have a chequered history, any ailment (like a history of mental illness or any form of disabilities)? If the findings turned out favourable, they would then approach the family of the girl, with their son. The girl's family will then call out the girl in question for everyone to see, entertain their guest and bid them farewell. Later, the girl's family will conduct their own investigations on the boy's family. If all goes well, they would then give their blessings for the union.

From the look of things, Dabo and Aima were not likely to find things easy in this respect. The most frustrating part of it was that they could not even discuss their relationships with their parents. Their parents disliked Petromina and were candid about it. In Aima's case, investigating Pierre's background would be extremely difficult.

* * * * * * *

Despite Aima's initial complaints about everything; ranging from the food vendors to the heat and filthy environment, she managed to settle in after the first week, although she still missed her French food and gym sessions.

Luckily, she found other means of exercise. She would wake up every morning and go to the nearest primary school field to jog. After jogging, she would go back home to a cold bath. Cold baths had never been this enjoyable to her. In fact, that was what they all grew up with. They never took warm baths.

She loved the school premises. Most mornings, she would sit on the cattle dung infested grass and watch the pupils as they go about school business. She reflected that any of the little school girls, in their tattered school uniforms could have been her. The difference was she never wore tattered clothes as her mum took special care of their school uniforms.

As a growing child, she had dreaded the harmattan season. It made the early morning bath water, cold as ice. For her, bathing was a pastime. She would first of all put the joy toilet soap in a bowl of water, rub the wet soap on her palms and then, apply it on her body like a lotion. Thereafter, she would close her eyes and pour the cold water all over her body at one go. Sometimes, she emerged from the bathroom with some parts of her body dry. In such instances, if she got caught, her mother took her back into the bathroom to give her a good scrub. Her teeth would chatter and her body shiver, but that never stopped Ibiye from pouring cold water over her body repeatedly as she scrubbed her with a rubber sponge.

Looking at the little girls in their school uniforms brought back happy memories. She remembered when it was her duty to empty the garbage bin. It used to be horrible. She would wake up early in the morning and attend to her assigned chores which included, sweeping and garbage disposal. She would sweep with eyes still laden with sleep, assemble the dirt and carry it in a bucket on her head to the designated (but unauthorized) waste disposal portion of the street. She too would add to the pile and dump hers' before running home.

Sometimes, she would see signs like 'don't dump refuse here'. When that happens, she would simply look to her left and right; if there were no adults in sight, she would drop the refuse and rush back home. If there were people around, she would cover a long distance on foot to look for the authorized refuse dump.

The garbage bins always stank. Most times, large ants crawled on her body from the bins when carried on her head. It used to be really horrible. But it was certainly better than when she and her siblings had to pick cow-dung from a cattle abattoir in the biting cold of the early morning. Their mum used the cow-dung as manure to grow vegetables, pepper, tomatoes, cassava and yam at their backyard.

Aima knew there was a better life but she never imagined there was anything like a hot bath. Inyingi loved enjoying life but it was a pity she did not live long enough to see her success. Aima would have given anything to save her life. She was like a second mother to her.

She was happy to hear Inyingi did not suffer before she died. She had been brave in the face of death. Her parents were by her bedside, when she died. She was told Inyingi had apologized to her family for whatever embarrassment and disgrace her wayward life had caused them. Aima got very emotional at the thought of Inyingi's name. Tears dripped down her eyes as she sat on the grass. A few pupils greeted as they passed by. One of them even asked if she was crying. In response, she shook her head, first to the left, and then to the right, before using her index finger to brush off the tears impatiently from her cheeks and smiled at the girl.

CHAPTER 15

Aima's stay in Nigeria was very fruitful. She had a family reunion, and before traveling back, was able to meet the basic needs of her family. Through Petromina's help, they were able to get a good bargain and replaced their rickety furniture with new ones at TBK Nigeria Limited. This singular effort endeared her to the Richardsons. Aima also bought the power generating set she had promised her dad, and also sold him the idea of having a hospital of his own. She promised to send him money periodically to complete the project.

Aima offered to take Moty along with her to France, but Moty declined the offer, citing serious ties she had in Nigeria. Aima suspected it might be a man but kept her suspicions to herself.

Fredrick gave up any hope of having more than a casual relationship with Petromina. He had seen the bond between her and Dabo blossom daily and wasn't prepared a cog in the wheel of progress even if it had cost him so much in time, finance, talent and other resources.

All of his adult life had been spent in the pursuit of mischief; some of which did astonish the Devil, and it's about time he made amends. He saw nothing wrong in starting now.

Miracle, his sister, felt he was mad for not pushing hard enough to get his desired woman, especially after the ordeal he'd put her through. She even suggested he threatened Petromina with a sack, but he disagreed because love is a matter of choice. What is more, she is very good at her job. The company needed people like her.

Petromina on her part, enrolled for a part-time programme in criminology. TBK gave incentives for any member of staff with the desire to better his lot academically. When her choice of course was known, they demanded she changed it, but she initially refused. Her experience in jail had informed her decision.

After about a year on the course, the company stopped paying for her tuition. They even made attending lectures difficult for her. They said that since her course of study had no bearing on the company's operations, it would be asinine to continue to sponsor her. Fredrick felt she might have an inkling of their business and it would be suicidal to help her study criminology of all courses. They gave her the option of changing her choice of course or lose her job.

She told her dilemma to Dabo who in turn, discussed it with his parents. This endeared her more to them because they knew no criminal would want to study criminology. They now believe there must be some good in her after all.

When asked why she chose the course, she answered that she hoped to contribute her quota to making Nigeria a better place by helping to rid the country of corruption. After all was said and done, there was nothing anyone can do for her, in the way of assistance. Not even Dabo or his family, on which she now pinned her hopes, could be of much help.

Dabo was neither engaged nor married to her, so they were not obliged to take up the huge responsibility of sponsoring her in school. As a matter of fact, Dabo had always told them he and Petromina were casual friends. She had no other choice but to change her course to Fine and Applied Arts.

Meanwhile, Aima had since returned to France and work. In a few months, she had sent her dad enough money to complete the hospital project. Despite her resistance, he named it 'Ima', meaning beauty. The full name is 'Ima, the beauty of Good Health Hospital.' An arm of the hospital is run by an NGO which provide free medical services for the under privileged in the society. People that fell into this category registered with the NGO and receive medication for free.

Aima was still not fulfilled in life. She has money, beauty and power and yet her happiness was partial. She craved complete happiness. She had prayed fervently and consistently for it and believed it would eventually come. In her dreams she still saw the treasure in the house of her childhood; could that be the secret of her joy? Could her happiness be in her own country and not in this land where everything was as beautiful as silver and gold? Time would tell!

*   *   *   *   *

Five years after Inyingi's death, her family could still not come to terms with it and were still grieving. Each of them felt responsible for her death in one way or the other.

Who today does not yearn for relief from the problems that face mankind; yet how often do our longings go unfulfilled? We dream of peace, but we cannot stem the rising tide of robbery, prostitution, rape and murder. We want to trust our neighbour, but we have to lock our doors for protection. We love our children and try to instill wholesome values in them, but all too often, we watch helplessly as they succumb to the unwholesome influence of their peers.

Still her parents reasoned that if they had paid a little more attention, they would have noticed her promiscuity. The warning signs were all there, but they were in denial. If only they had been more firm, more resolute against her wantonness, perhaps, she would still be alive today. If only they had not spared the rod, their daughter would not have ended up a trollop. If they... Oh, the hopelessness of it all!

Her siblings on their part felt they should have alerted their parents. Like a scene from a horror movie, they recalled with frightening clarity, the uncountable times Inyingi had bribed them with presents so they wouldn't tell on her. They had readily accepted these gifts even when their hearts had vehemently protested. They were indeed culpable even if they were then ignorant of the futility and sometimes fatality, of promiscuity.

The family agreed to hold a memorial seminar, exactly on the 5th year memorial of her death.

Public speakers were invited and so were a host of others; parents and youths alike for the event.

Aima flew in from Paris a night before the ceremony. She had a lot of work and her office could afford only to give her four days off. She decided to arrive just a day earlier so she could rest and spend the remaining days with her family before going back to Paris. Her parents gave her the details on what the seminar would entail and what the highpoints would be.

As they entered the auditorium, Inyingi's photographs were enlarged and conspicuously hung at strategic corners. Immediately Aima saw the picture, tears came rolling down her cheeks uncontrollably. She sat with the invited guests; where nobody would notice her presence. It could be embarrassing to sit at the family reserved area and then cry uncontrollably for everybody to see.

The programme for the day was circulated. It read: A Seminar in Memory of Inyingi Richardson (1950 – 1975). Theme: The Effects of Promiscuity.

Agenda:

1   Opening Prayer by Rev. Kanu
2   Introduction of the Chairman and Special Guests by the MC
3   Lecture by various speakers
4   Questions, answers and contributions
5   Launching of Inyingi Foundation for single and unemployed girls
6   Sale of memorial souvenirs
7   Refreshment and music
8   Closing remarks by the Governor of Rivers State

Aima could barely go through the content of the programme. Her tears continued to flow. Meanwhile, the family was confused. They knew she was at the auditorium but she was not sitting with them. They wondered where she could be and Angel was sent to go and look for her. She came back and told them Aima was seated with the invited guests.

The programme went well as expected. The speakers delved deep into the dangers of promiscuity. They all agreed there was no advantage in the act and appealed to youths to desist from it. They were advised to abstain from sex, but if they could not resist, they should ensure they used condoms. They were also told oral sex was also sex which had its own condoms. Many spoke. One agreed that some people were lucky and would not contact any disease but concluded that: "This one time beauty queen is no more." Speaker after speaker pointed to the picture of late Inyingi. "Whenever you want to fornicate, remember the face of this beauty that is no more amongst us." They generally advised.

Finally, it was time for the State Governor to speak. He had however sent his deputy to represent him. Aima still had her face in her hands, crying. She did not look up throughout the time the other speakers addressed the audience neither did she pay attention to their names or their utterances. As the Deputy Governor, Eddy Richmond, walked to the rostrum, his presence filled the room. As he began to speak, Aima had a certain sensation. The voice was a familiar one. She looked up and trembled.

"Good heavens! I can't believe my eyes." She wiped her eyes and pinched herself to make sure she was not having one of those funny dreams again. It seemed to her that his life had just begun. "Has he always been this handsome? He is definitely looking younger and taller."

As his admirers commented around her, it became clear to Aima that Richmond was indeed the person she was seeing. Her bewilderment knew no bounds. As the Governor was unavoidably absent, he had sent Richmond to deputize for him.

While Aima continued to listen she decided to catch up with him at the end of the ceremony before he disappeared with his entourage.

"Inyingi was personally known to me." She heard him say. "The Governor did me a great favour by asking me to represent him at this occasion. People should not remember Inyingi for her promiscuity only. We are here to learn how her example could change our lives. There were many good sides to her. Her inside was as pretty as her outside. She was also a hardworking lady. Every youth should remember it pays to work hard." He continued, his next statement striking Aima dumb. "What we all need is the fear of God. The fear of God is the beginning of wisdom. If we fear and love God, promiscuity will fly away and good things shall come our way naturally.

"The moral perfidy of our youths today may be ascribed to parental negligence. The uncertainty of existence and the individualism of contemporary times have ushered in new lows in our moral standards. In fact, we have watered down our moral standards to the point where many of our youths are confused, discouraged and in deep trouble. We are now reaping the harvest of parental neglect, divorce, child abuse, school drop-outs, illegal drugs and streets full of violence. If only our parents would be more responsible, our homes would be more peaceful and the society safer and better. And our young ladies should comport themselves properly. They should dress decently and appropriately, not revealing what should be concealed. Hear this, and hear it well; there is always someone for everyone. We can't all be saints but we should endeavour to put in our very best in life and leave the world, better than we found it. In a nutshell, we should stop majoring on the minors and minoring on the majors."

He paused, took a sip from his glass of water, and then continued:

"I once had a friend who told me her body was the temple of God and not a toy for men to play with. I didn't act like a noble then."

Aima shuddered; she knew she was the friend he was referring to.

Richmond continued: "Today, I am happy that God had forgiven me all my sins. What about you? Have you confessed your sins to God? If not, when will you do that? Tomorrow may be too late. As we have been told here, Inyingi gave her life to Christ on her hospital bed. Not everyone may have the grace or opportunity to do that. I know this is not a church service but you can call me up anytime and I will gladly lead you to Christ. Thank you all and God bless."

There was a long round of applause. Aima could neither believe her eyes nor ears. She wondered if Richmond would recognize her if she accosted him.

The chairman of the occasion immediately appealed to Richmond to give the closing prayer and invitees were asked to remain seated until the Deputy Governor made his exit.

Immediately after the prayers, Aima stood up to meet him, but her legs wobbled. Richmond, who had been curious as to why Aima was absent at such a widely publicized event was suddenly attracted to her figure. The last he had heard of her was when she was in Lagos, during her National Youth Service. He walked towards her, like one in a trance.

"Hi," he said. "My name is Richmond. Who are you?"

"I am Aima, Aima Richardson."

"And what does the beautiful name mean?"

"Beauty!" She replied with a chuckle.

"Tobura?" He asked how she was doing in Kalabari language.

"Ibim!" She laughingly replied that she was fine.

Aima knew there and then that she had and would always be in love with him, but the 'bridge' that was between them had become even longer over the years.

"Come with me!" He said.

"No!" She replied shyly.

"My intentions are noble, please come home with me"

"No!" She again declined.

"I am very harmless. You can ask my boys."

Richmond tried to persuade her and this time, in response, she shook her head.

"Don't shake your head," he pleaded. "People are watching us."

"Okay your Excellency. I will go with you."

Aima visited Richmond privately after the ceremony but due to official engagements they could not discuss at length and so, he invited her to lunch the next day at Government House.

After a simple meal, consisting of fried plantain, eggs and Quaker oats, served personally by the chef of government house, Richmond led her away from the dinning room to an adjoining lounge.

Aima could tell something big was about to happen but could not put her finger on it. Whatever it was, she prayed it won't waste her time; she had only a day left before returning to Paris.

"Aima, my dearest Aima. Seeing you again after so many years was like rain after a long and hard dry season. You are a breath of fresh air to my soul." Richmond declared.

Aima remained silent, not sure where this declaration will lead.

"I have thought of you every single second of everyday," he continued. "You are the best thing that has ever happened to me, and may God bless the day I met you."

Aima became fidgety, sure now as to the drift of his diatribe.

"My dearest, I had you once but foolishly let you slip out of my hands. Ladies like you are difficult to come by, especially in these days where moral rectitude sounds obnoxious to many a youth. I don't intend to lose you again, especially now that circumstances are favourable."

"How do you mean?" Aima asked, still uncomfortable.

"My wife lost her life back in the United States in a natural disaster which came in the shape of a hurricane some years ago and has since been buried. Constance has also left my house and life out of anger for my reluctance to formalize our relationship. She left with her kids."

Aima sat still, knowing what would come next. He certainly had laid a good foundation!

"Please marry me, Aima. I promise to love and cherish you, to cherish and love you all the days of my life. My life will amount to nothing without you."

He searched her face for any tell-tale sign, saw none and then continued.

"This proposal I have made in cognizance of all the things I hold dear and sacred. I am a changed man; not given to debauchery as before. I will give you my very life if only you will be my wife."

Aima was confused. She found herself in the horns of dilemma.

"Should I return to the lights of Paris and work or shelve all I had worked so hard to achieve for a life as Mrs. Aima Richmond Jnr.?" She wondered.

Richmond, who had been waiting for an answer, coughed to bring her back to earth.

Congruent with her nature, Aima took her time before answering.

"Dear Eddy, I am flattered by your proposal, truly I am. I had loved you all my adult life, and in fact, you remain the only man I had truly loved. But as you know, marriage traverses the couples; it involves families."

Richmond, all ears, waited for her to finish.

"What is more, there are issues, plenty of issues I would like to address before giving you my answer. You see, I wasn't exactly living in a nunnery since we parted ways! A lot has happened and I pray you give me time to gather myself."

"I understand what you are driving at," he said with feeling. "I will give you enough time to tidy up your affairs. Take your time and tie up every loose end. I have heard good things always come to those who wait and I am prepared to wait for you."

With that, he walked her down to the parking lot and ordered his driver to drop her at home.

Weary from the exertions of the day, she retired to bed early and dreamt.

In her dream, the scene of a shaky bridge had disappeared and had been replaced by that of a treasure in her roots; in the house of her childhood. She was smiling as she woke up.

"Could Richmond be the treasure?" She wondered. "And what about Pierre, what do I do about him? And what about my own story I wanted to write?"

She wished her late sister, Inyingi, was there to assist her in this stalemate.

"Which way should I go, Inyingi? My left leads to Paris and all it entails and my right to Richmond. Which way should I go? Tell me, guide me, tell me, advise me…"

Like rain after a long spell of harmattan, she seemed to hear her late sister's refreshing response.

"I have never shared your views, but this time I will. Follow your mind, Aima! Follow your mind! Grab your treasure! Your treasure are in your hands, grab them! Grab your treasures…!"

THE END